HAL•LEONARD
GUITAR
PLAY-ALONG

AUDIO
ACCESS
INCLUDED

CONTENTS

Page	Title
2	The Ballad of John Henry
14	Dust Bowl
23	If Heartaches Were Nickels
56	Last Kiss
79	Lonesome Road Blues
38	Sloe Gin
88	So, It's Like That
97	So Many Roads, So Many Trains
112	GUITAR NOTATION LEGEND

To access audio visit:
www.halleonard.com/mylibrary

Enter Code
4499-4244-0054-2446

Cover photo: Jerome Brunet

ISBN 978-1-60378-426-9

Visit Hal Leonard Online at
www.halleonard.com

The Ballad of John Henry

Words and Music by Joe Bonamassa

*Tune down 2 1/2 steps:
(low to high) B-E-A-D-F#-B

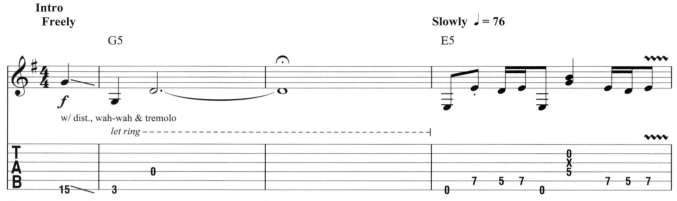

*Baritone gtrs. arr. for standard gtr. (music sounds a 4th lower than indicated).

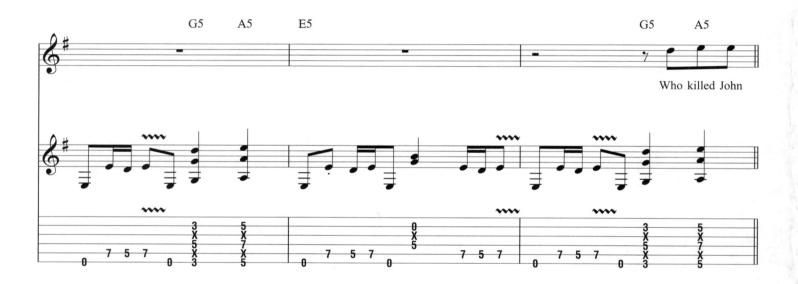

Who killed John

Chorus

Hen - ry   in the bat - tle of sin - ners and

saints?   Who killed John   Hen - ry

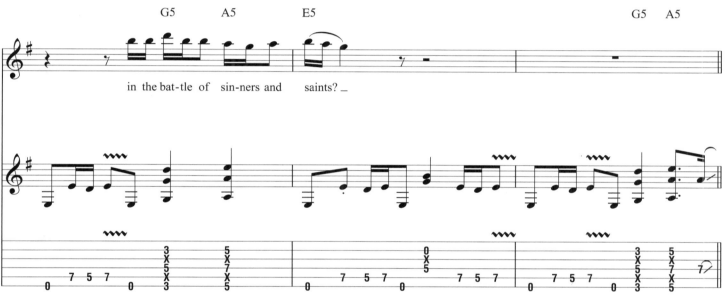

in the bat - tle of   sin - ners and   saints? _

Verse

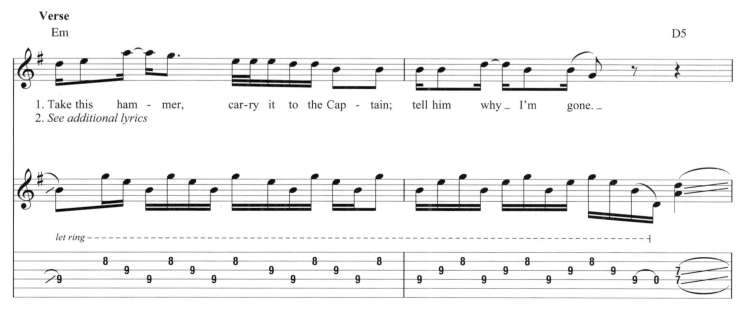

1. Take this   ham - mer,   car - ry it to the Cap - tain;   tell him   why _ I'm   gone. _
2. *See additional lyrics*

let ring - ⌐

3

Take this ham - mer, car-ry it to the Cap - tain; tell him I'm __ go - in' home. __ I don't

want your __ cold i - ron shack-les a - round my __ leg. __ I don't

want your __ cold i - ron shack-les a - round my __ leg. __ Who killed John

Give me the ham - mer that killed John Hen-ry 'cause it won't _ kill _____ me. Who killed John

Chorus

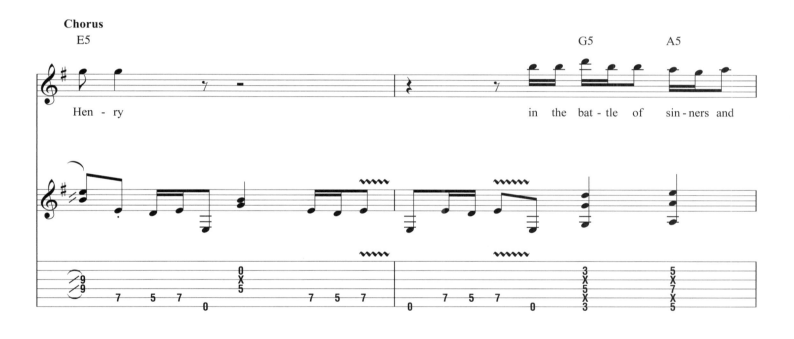

Hen - ry   in the bat - tle   of   sin - ners   and

saints?   Who killed John   Hen - ry

in the bat-tle of sin-ners and saints? _

Mm. _____

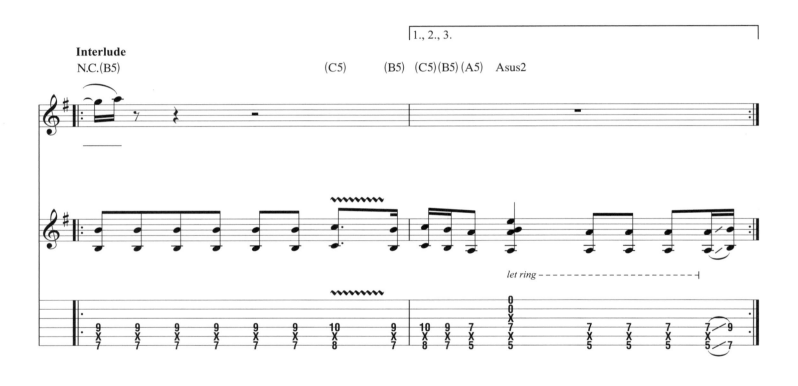

Interlude

1., 2., 3.

let ring -

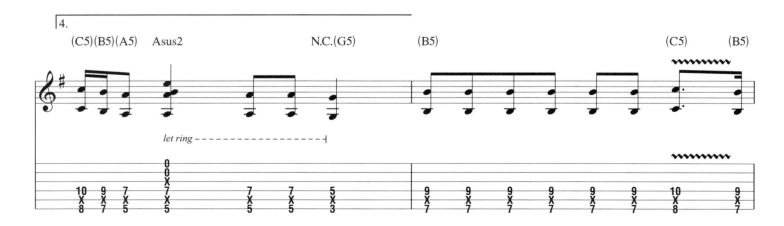

4.

let ring - - - - - - - - - - - - - - - - -

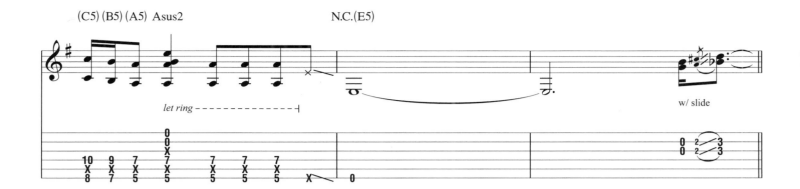

Guitar Solo

N.C.(E5)

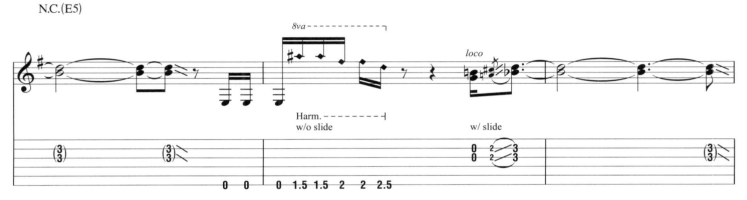

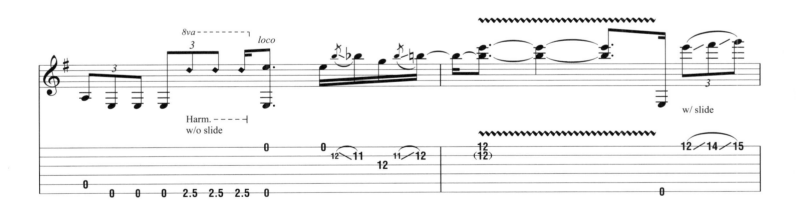

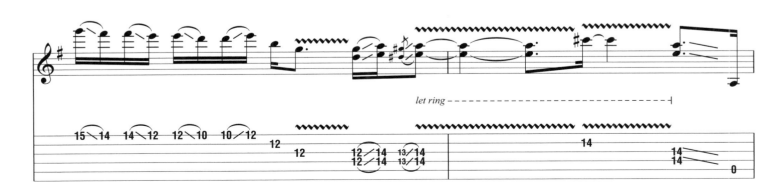

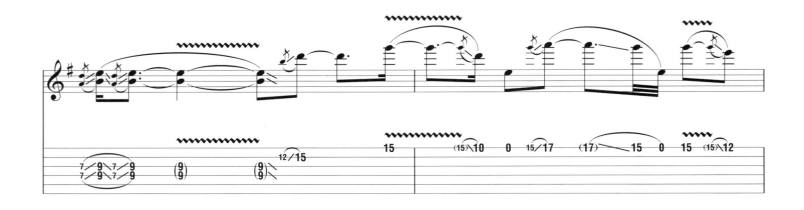

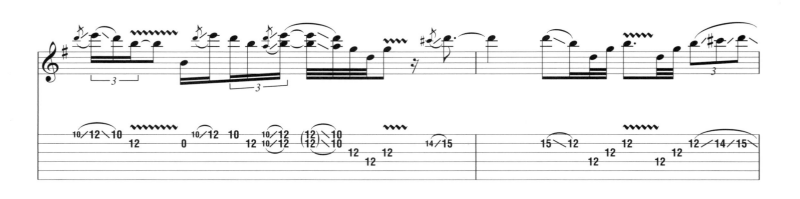

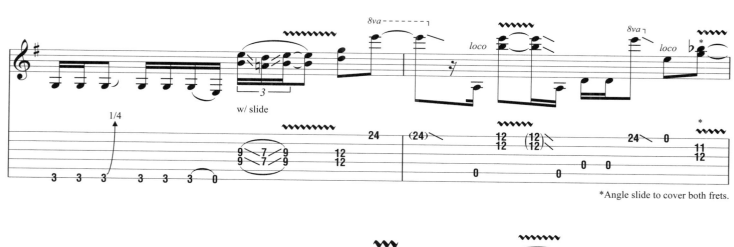

*Angle slide to cover both frets.

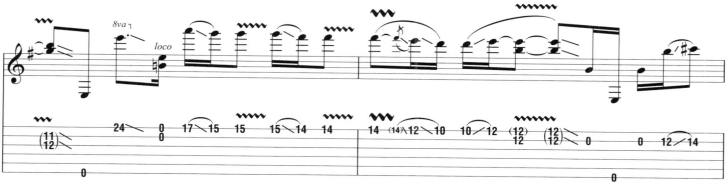

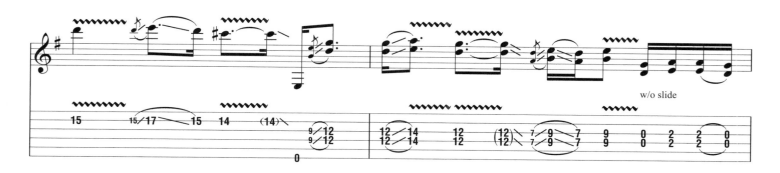

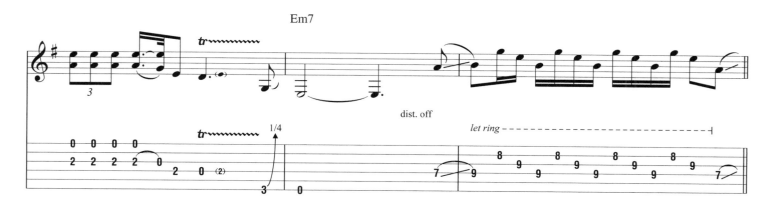

9

Verse

3. Take this ham - mer, car-ry it to the Cap - tain; tell him I'm __ go - in' home. __

Take this ham - mer, car-ry it to the Cap - tain; tell him why __ I'm gone. __ I'm a

want-ed man with the Cap - tain. __ I'm a want - ed man in the shack - les.

I'm a want - ed man in the shack - les. I'm a want - ed man. ___ Who killed John

Chorus

Hen - ry in the bat-tle of sin-ners and saints?

Who killed John Hen - ry in the bat-tle of sin-ners and

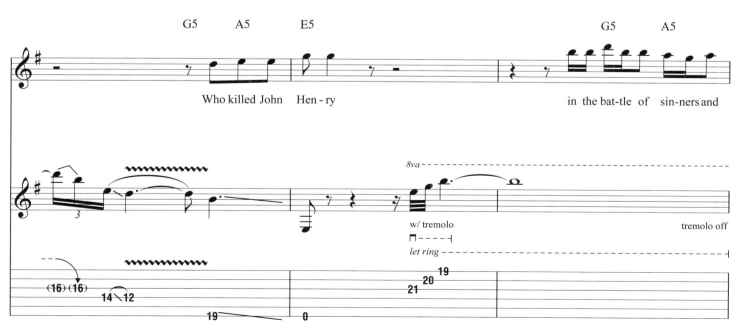

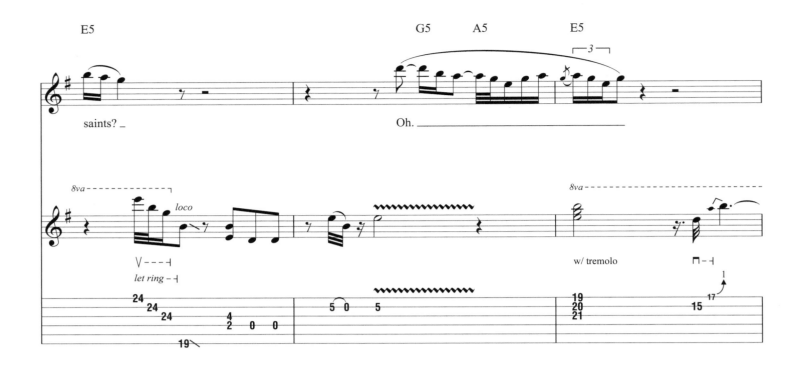

saints? _

Oh. _____

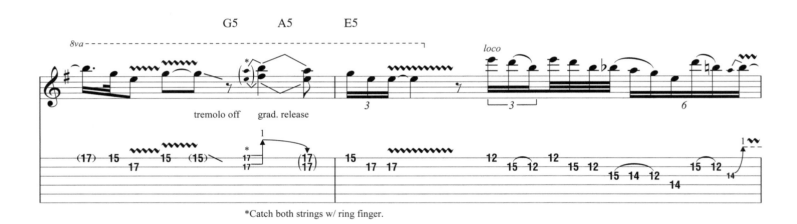

*Catch both strings w/ ring finger.

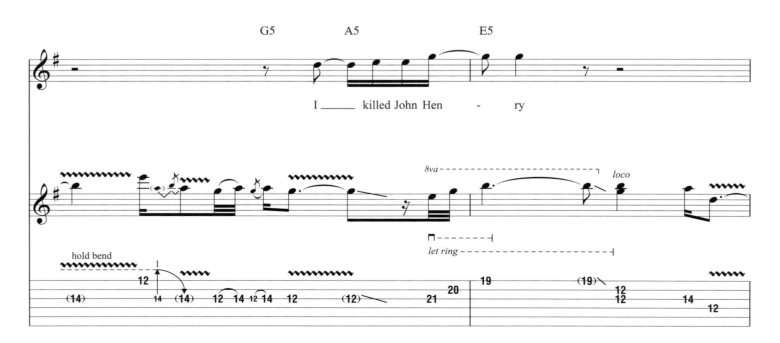

I ____ killed John Hen - ry

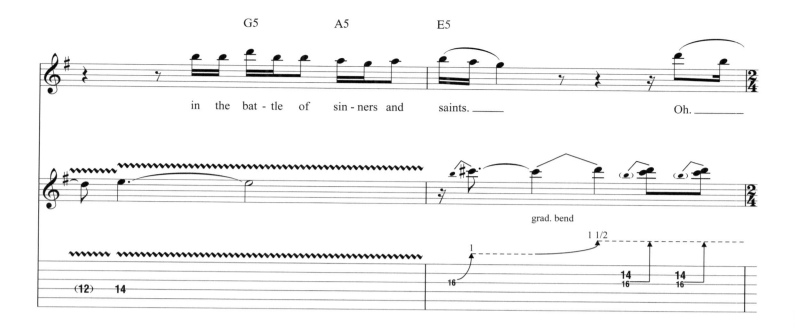

in the bat - tle of sin - ners and saints. _____ Oh. _____

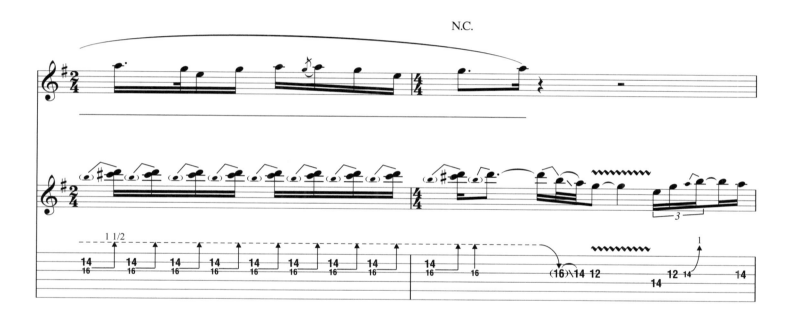

Repeat and fade

Additional Lyrics

2. I'm a long way from Colorado, a long way from my home.
Get the hammer that killed John Henry; won't kill me no more.
Give me the hammer that killed John Henry 'cause it won't kill me.
Give me the hammer that killed John Henry 'cause it won't kill me.

Dust Bowl

Words and Music by Joe Bonamassa

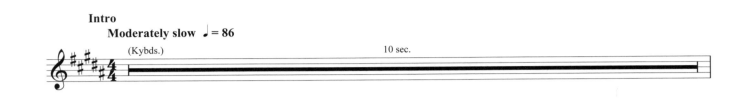

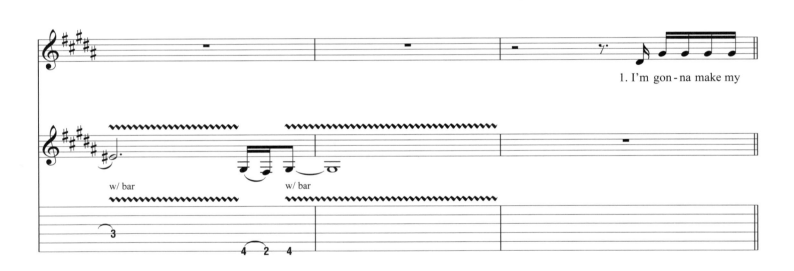

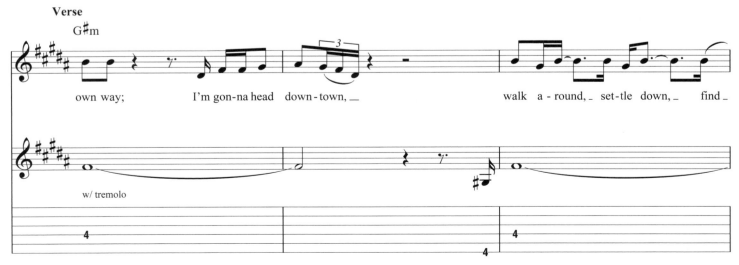

me a prop-er drink.   Don't need a hel - met   to get me through life. _   I

tremolo off

w/ bar

walk a - cross _ the wa - ter;   blame _ it on fool-ish pride. _   Lift-ing me up, _

w/ bar

reverb off

% Chorus

G#5   F#5   G#5   F#5

— _   tear - ing me down. _____   All _

w/ dist.

you give me is in-de-ci-sion, the clas-sic run-a-round. Bring-ing me high-

-er, keep-ing me whole. Now

To Coda 1 ⊕
To Coda 2 ⊕

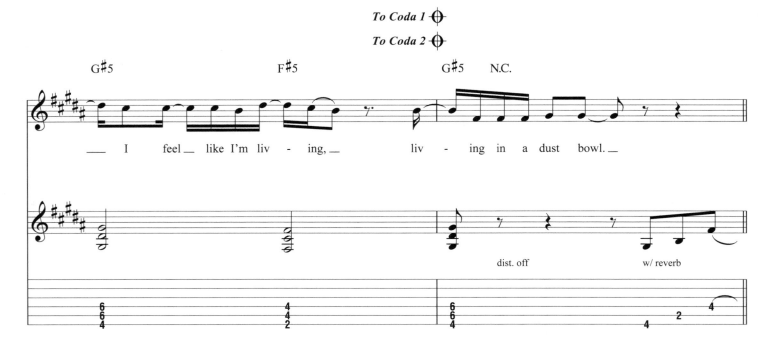

I feel like I'm liv-ing, liv-ing in a dust bowl.

dist. off   w/ reverb

Interlude

2. Dia-monds and

Verse

pearls, ___ you're that kind of girl. ___ You

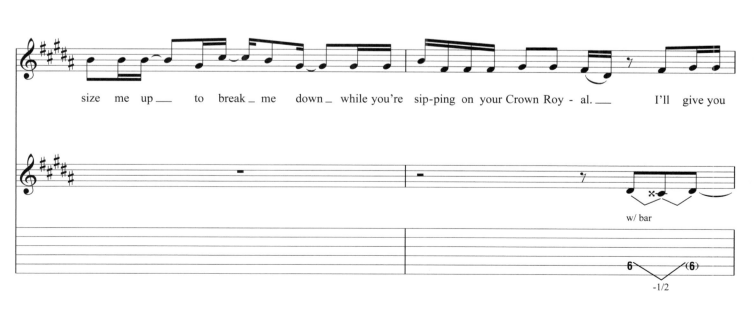

size me up __ to break _ me down _ while you're sip-ping on your Crown Roy - al. ___ I'll give you

shel - ter;   babe; it's your   call. __   It's

D.S. al Coda 1

Gtr. tacet

hard   to   find __   truth __ with - in __ when you're liv - ing in your own   zone. __   Lift - ing me up, __

⊕ Coda 1

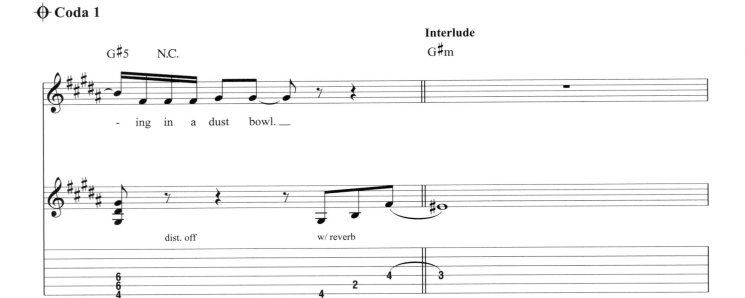

G#5   N.C.   **Interlude**
                                          G#m

- ing   in   a   dust   bowl. __

dist. off   w/ reverb

Harm.

+1/2

*Bend behind nut.

Guitar Solo

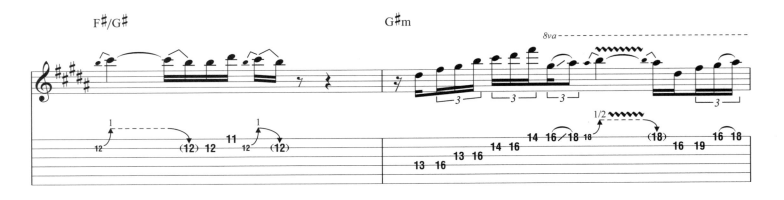

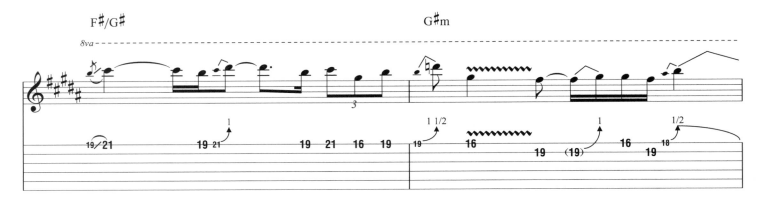

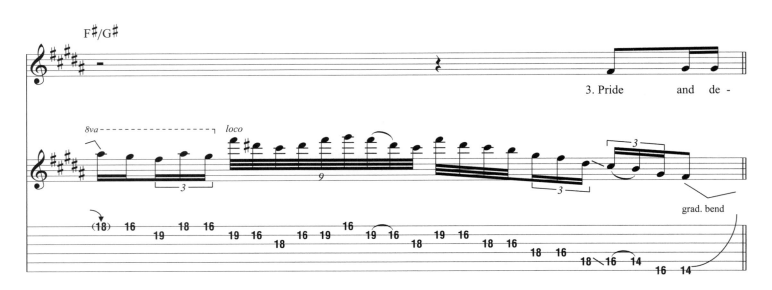

3. Pride and de-

Verse

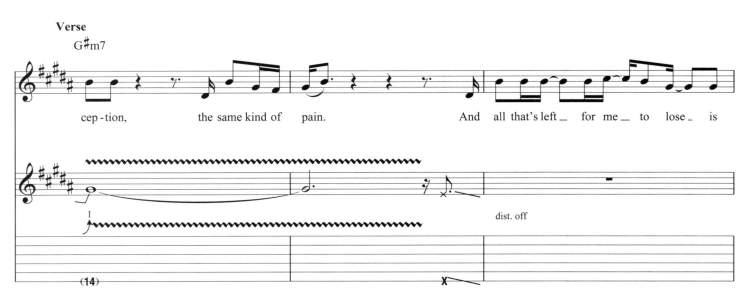

cep-tion,   the same kind of pain.   And   all that's left_ for me _ to lose_ is

dist. off

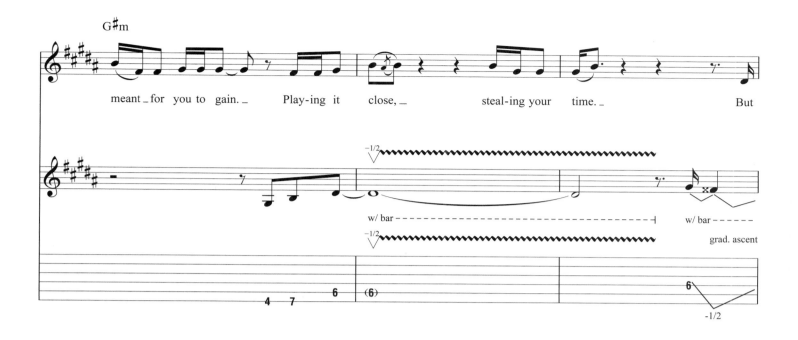

meant _ for you to gain. _ Play-ing it close, _ steal-ing your time. _ But

D.S. al Coda 2

who cares _ an - y - way? I've gone _ the ex - tra mile. _ Lift -ing me up, _

 Coda 2

Outro

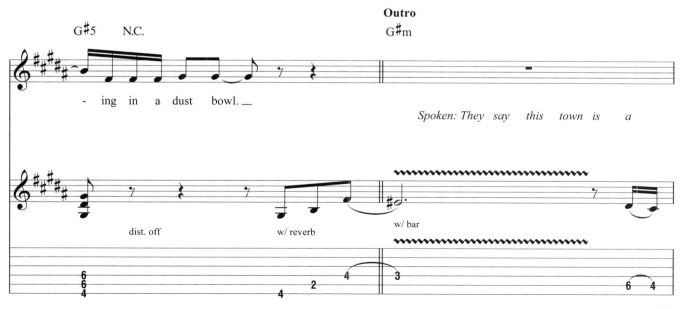

- ing in a dust bowl. _

Spoken: They say this town is a

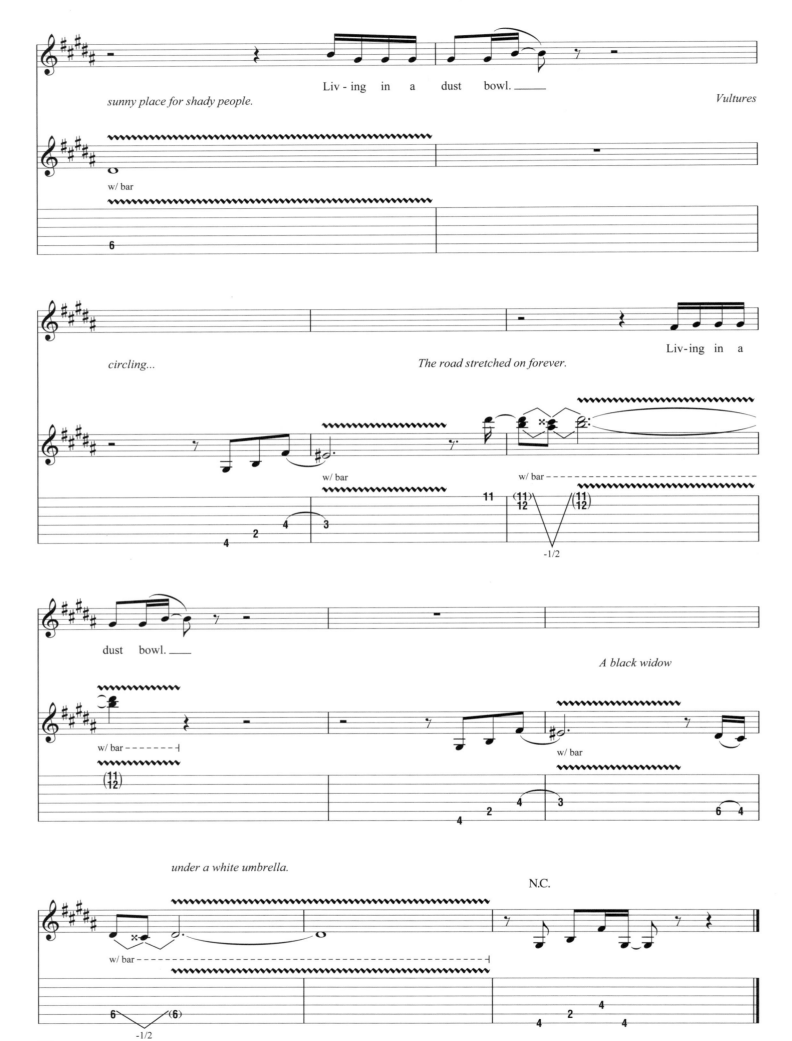

sunny place for shady people.

Liv - ing in a dust bowl. ____

Vultures

circling...

The road stretched on forever.

Liv - ing in a

dust bowl. ____

A black widow

under a white umbrella.

N.C.

If Heartaches Were Nickels

Words and Music by Warren Haynes

Tune down 1/2 step:
(low to high) Eb-Ab-Db-Gb-Bb-Eb

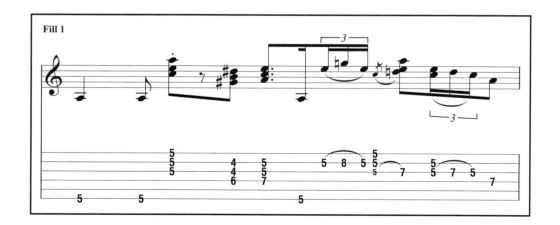

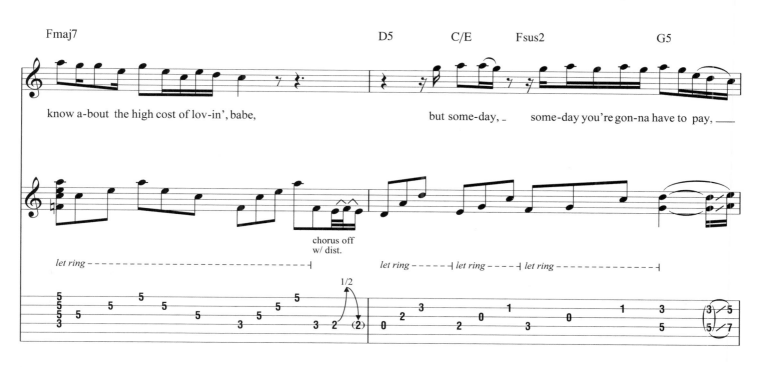

𝄋 Bridge

2nd time, substitute Fill 2

wine _____ and pills were hun-dred dol-lar bills, I might keep you _ sat-is-fied. _____ And if

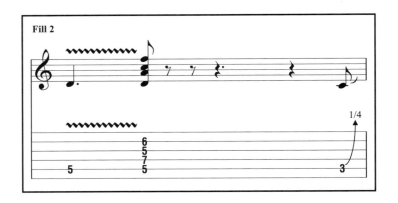

Fill 2

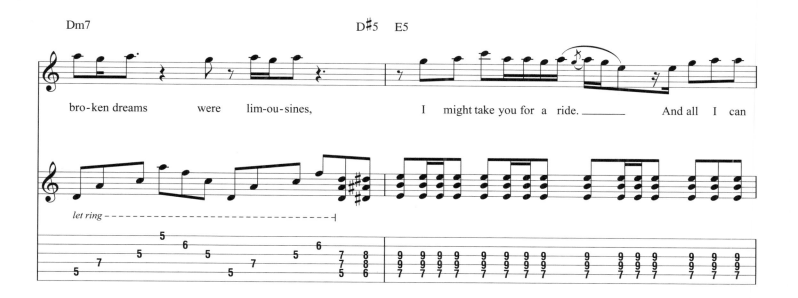

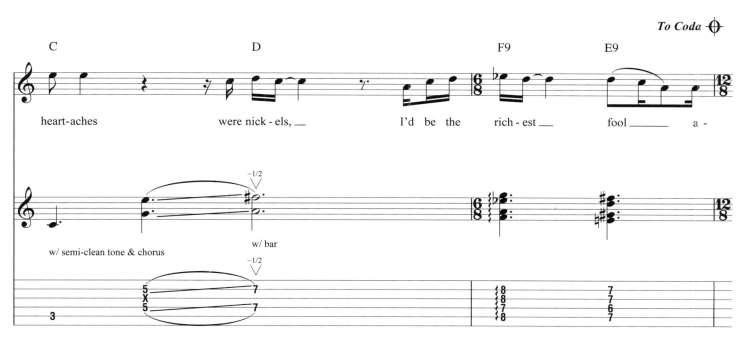

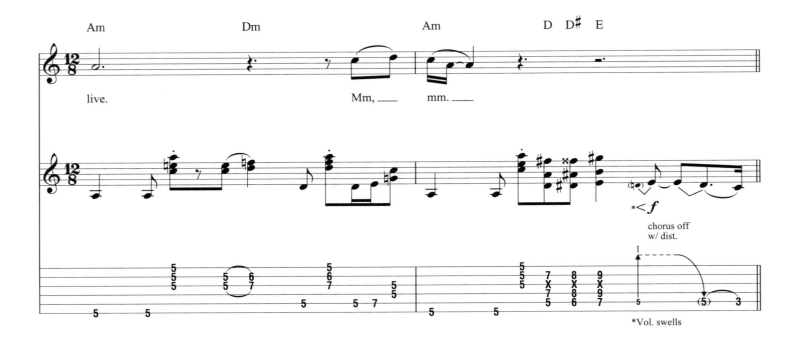

Guitar Solo

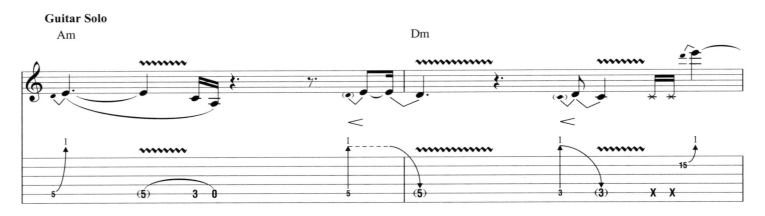

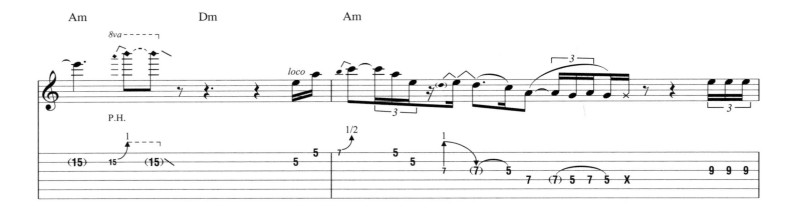

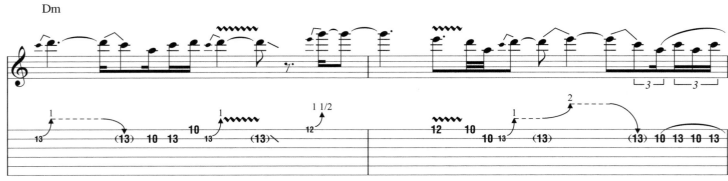

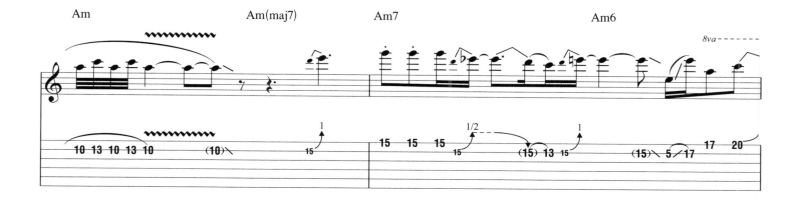

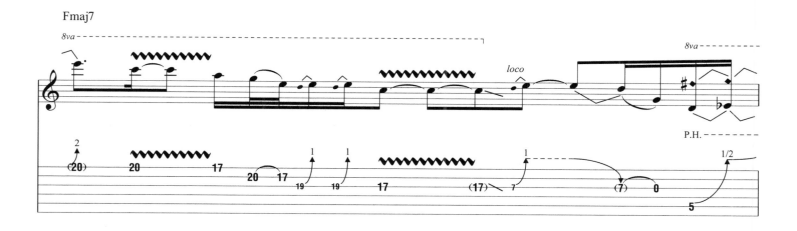

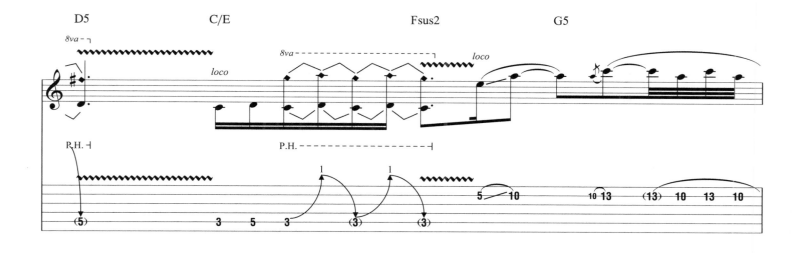

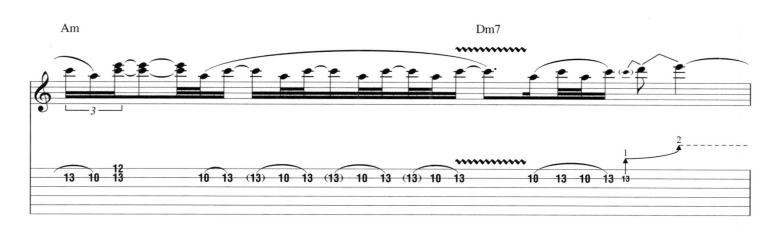

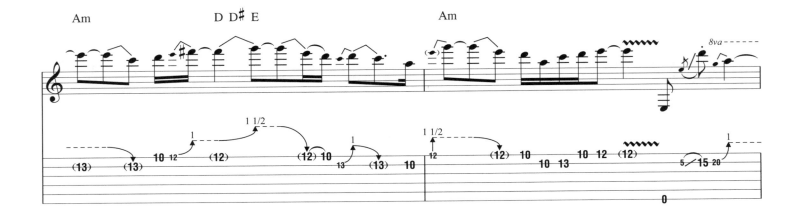

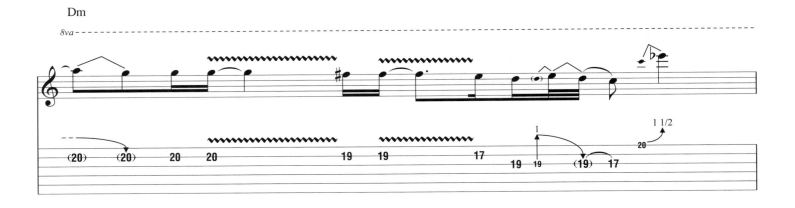

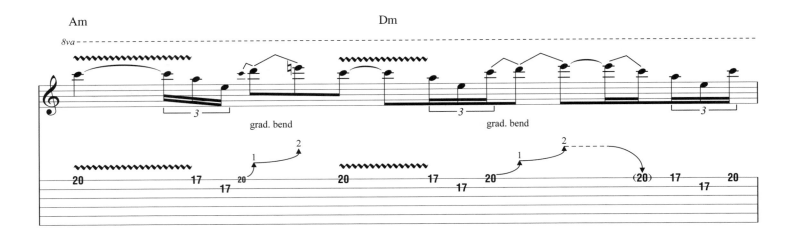

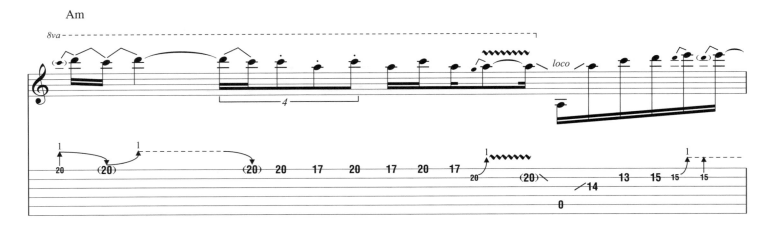

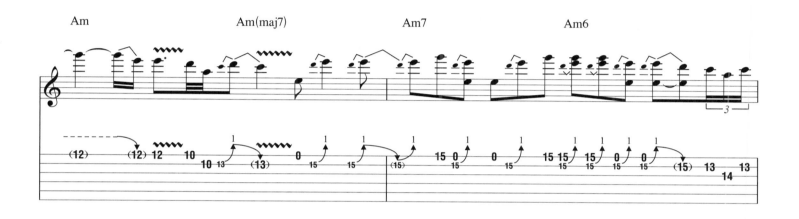

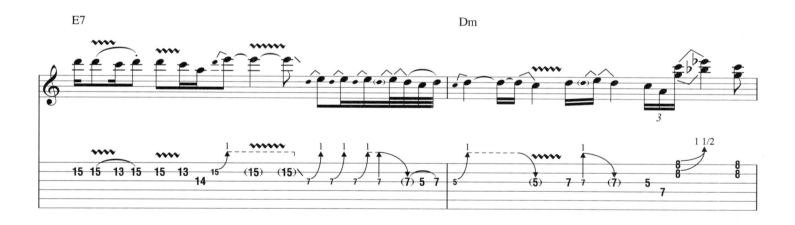

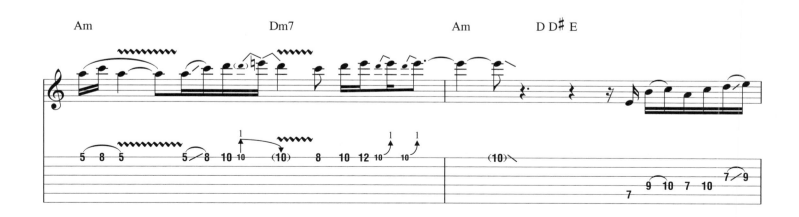

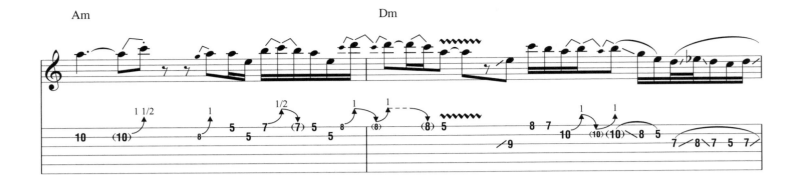

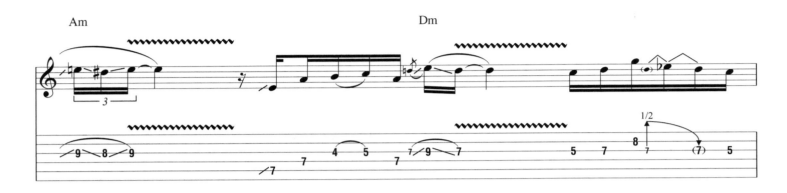

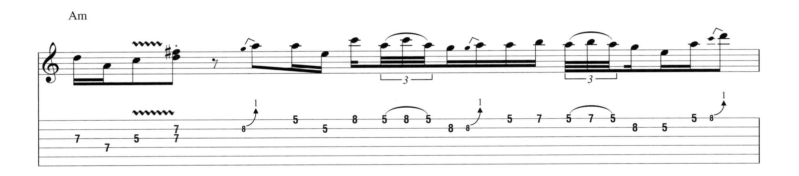

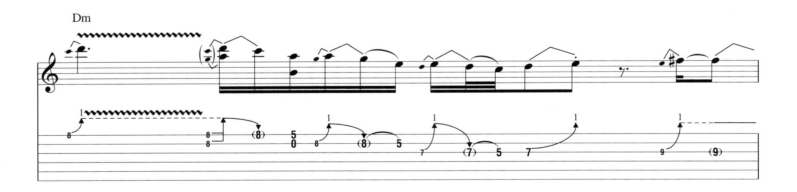

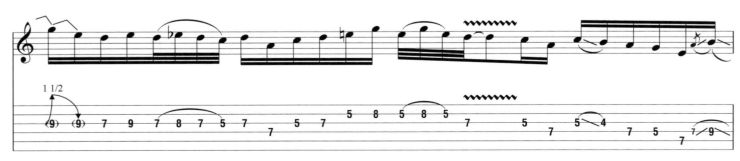

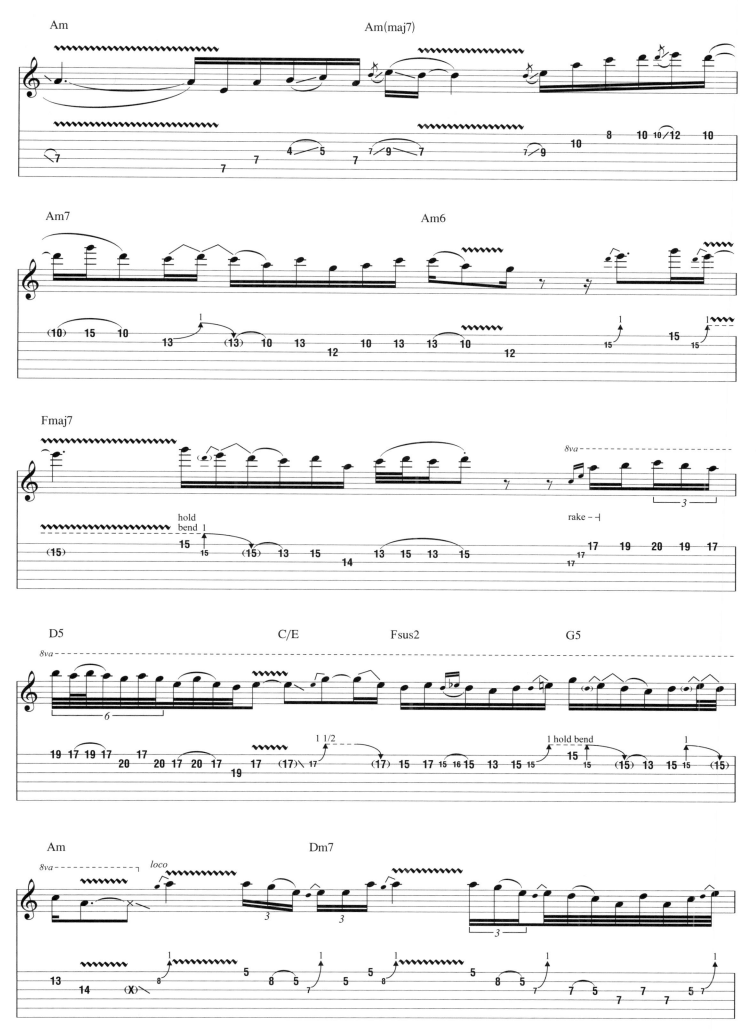

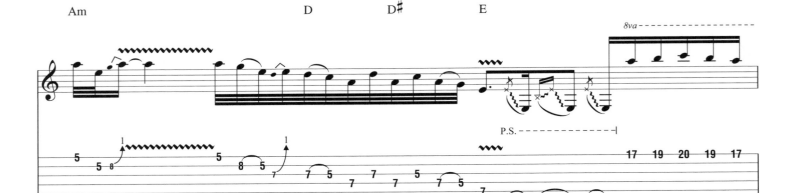

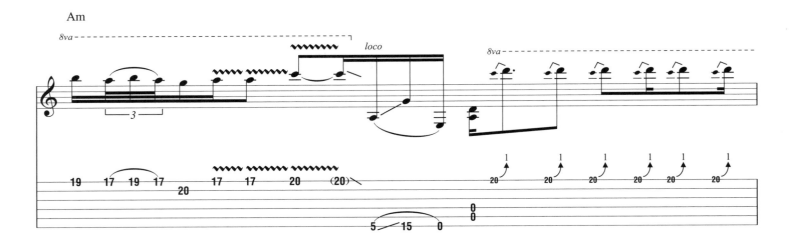

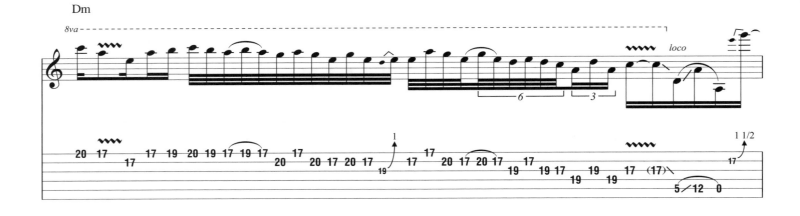

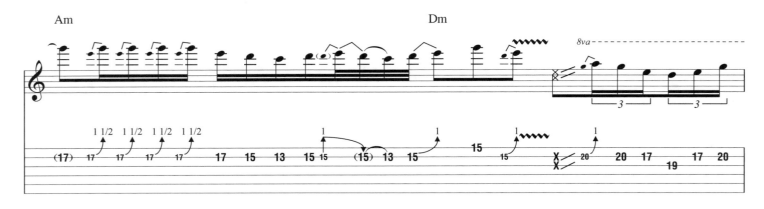

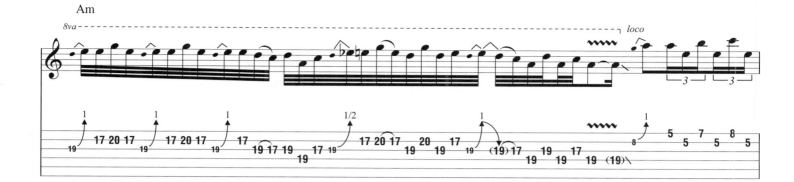

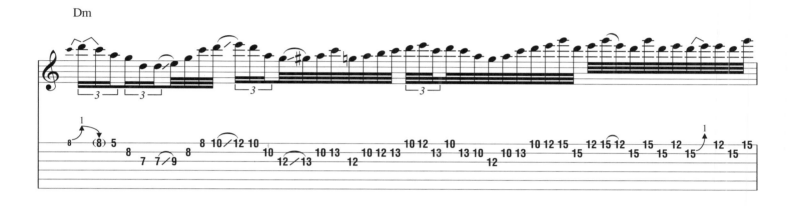

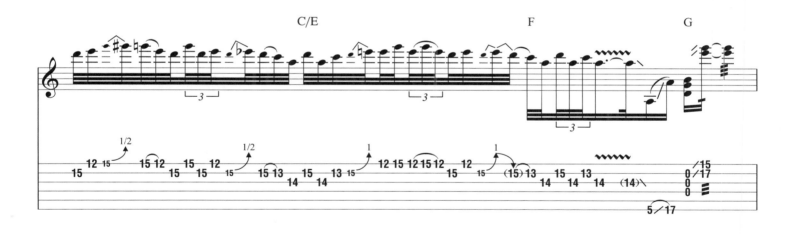

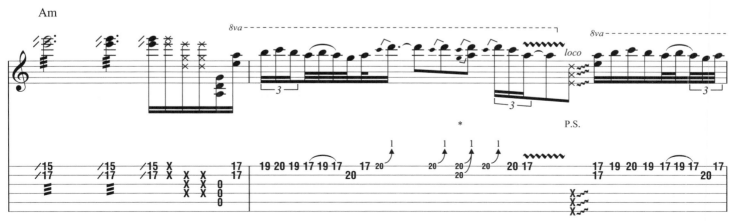

*Bend both notes w/ same finger.

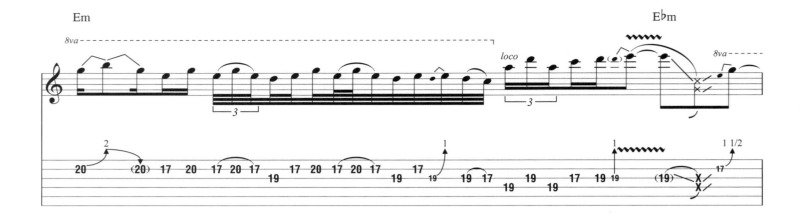

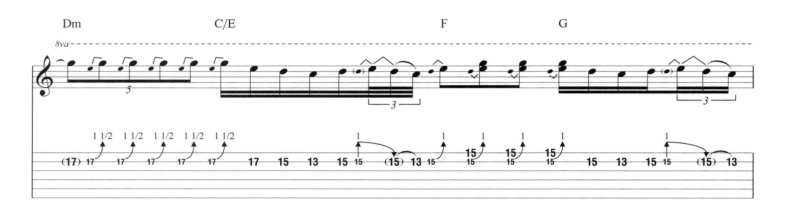

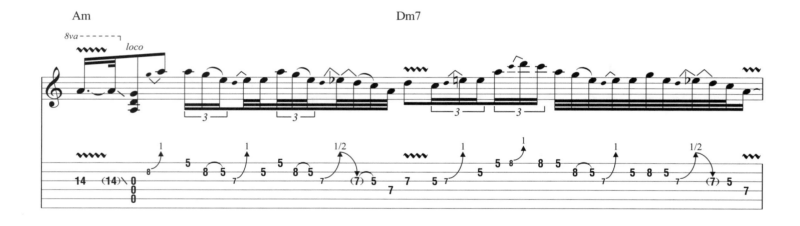

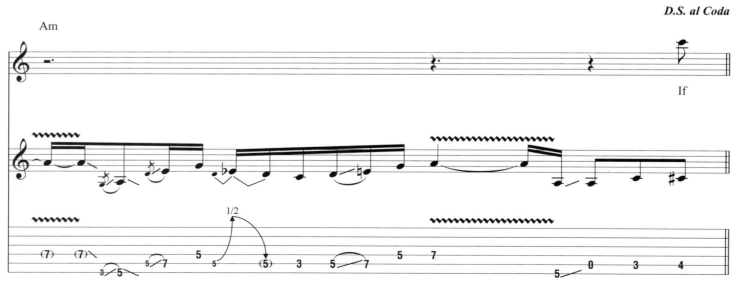

⊕ Coda

live,

I'd ___ be the rich-est fool a - live. _____

Freely

Am7

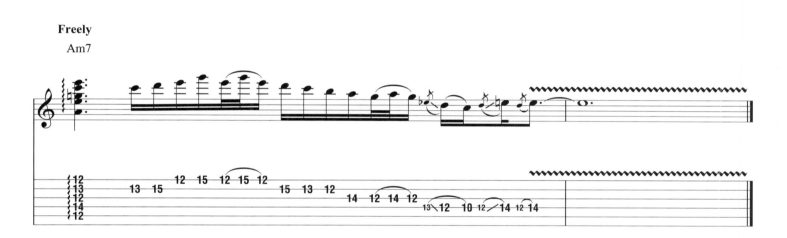

Additional Lyrics

2. Well, a woman like you needs fine things,
   And I knew it from the start.
   And I don't have much to offer,
   Just this old broken heart,
   Yeah, baby, just this old broken heart.
   But if heartaches were nickels,
   I would not, I wouldn't be here cryin' in the dark.

Sloe Gin

Words and Music by Bob Ezrin and Michael Kamen

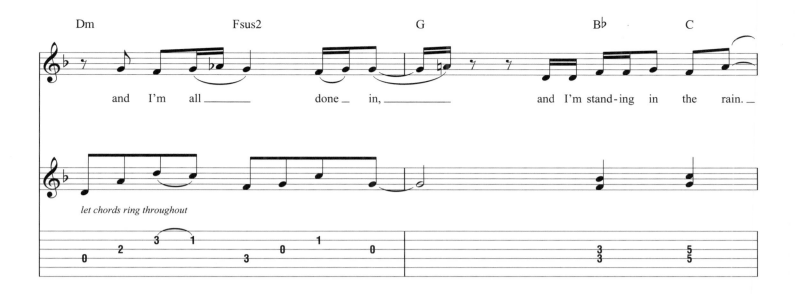

and I'm all _____ done _ in, _____ and I'm stand-ing in the rain. _

let chords ring throughout

_____ And I feel _____ like I'm gon-na cry. _____

Chorus

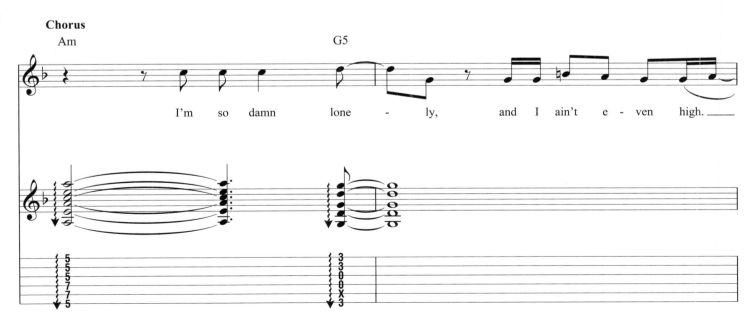

I'm so damn lone - ly, and I ain't e - ven high. _____

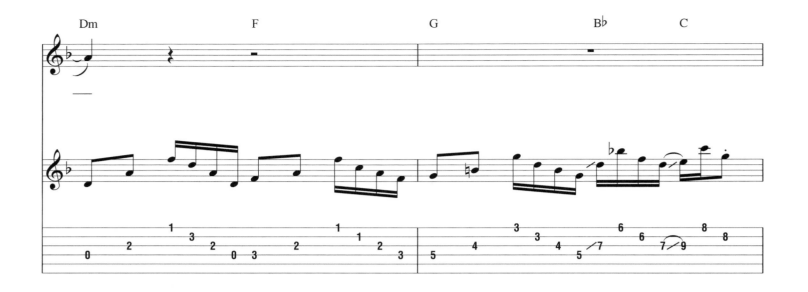

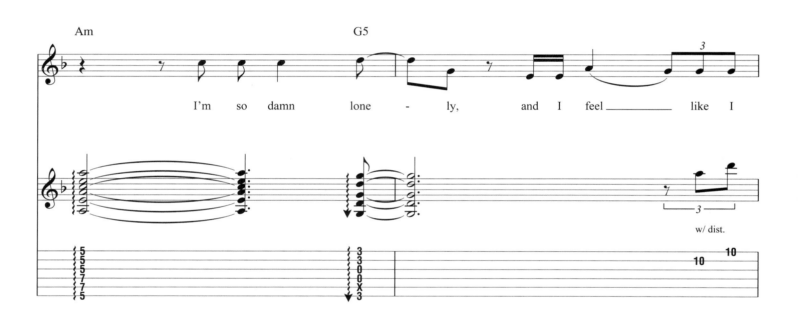

I'm so damn lone - ly, and I feel _____ like I

w/ dist.

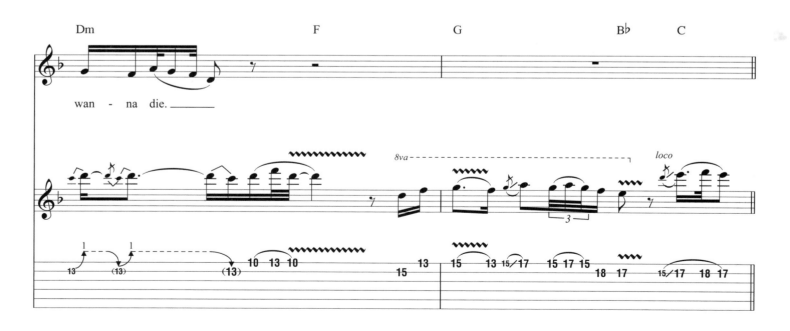

wan - na die. _____

*Using a guitar with Les Paul style electronics, set lead volume to 10 and rhythm volume to 0. Strike the strings while the pickup selector switch is in the lead position, then flip the switch in the rhythm indicated to simulate the re-attack.

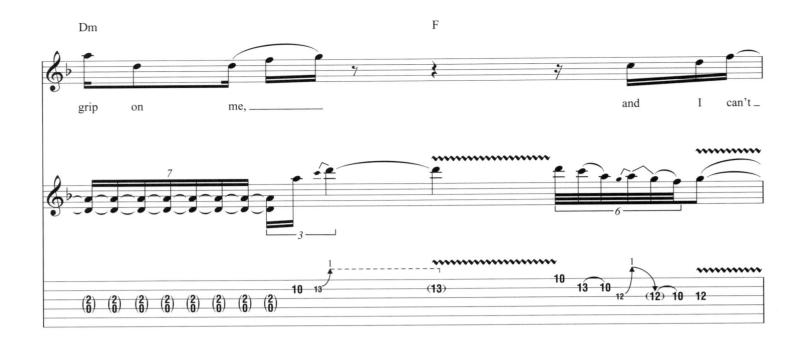

grip on me, _____ and I can't _

Chorus

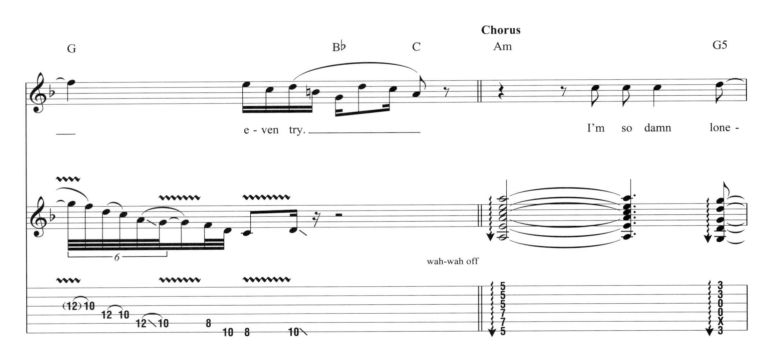

e - ven try. _____ I'm so damn lone -

wah-wah off

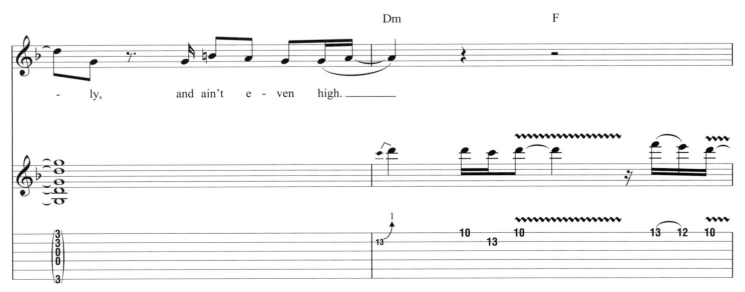

- ly, and ain't e - ven high. _____

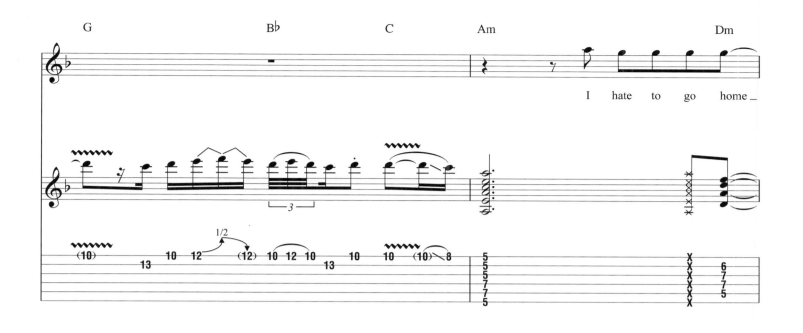

I hate to go home _

_ a - lone, __ but what else _____ is new?

let ring -

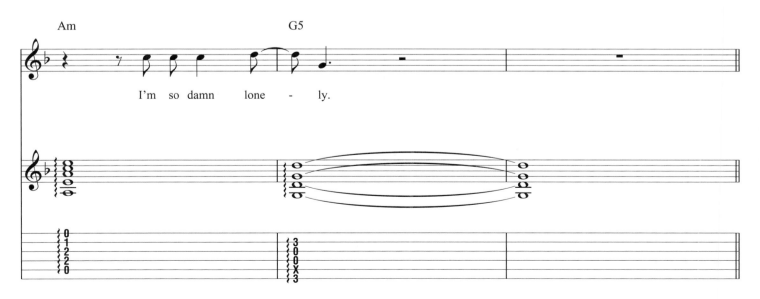

I'm so damn lone - ly.

Guitar Solo

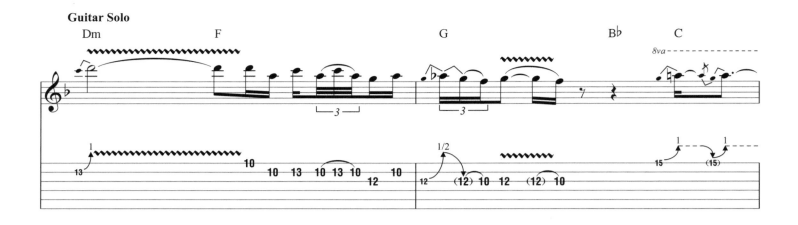

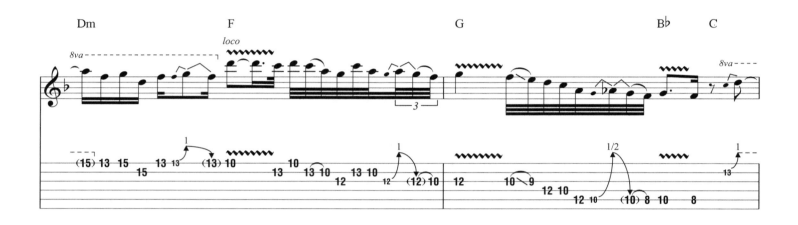

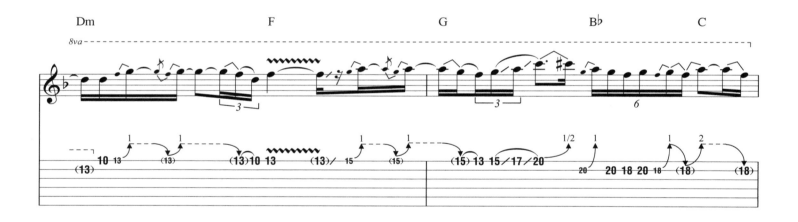

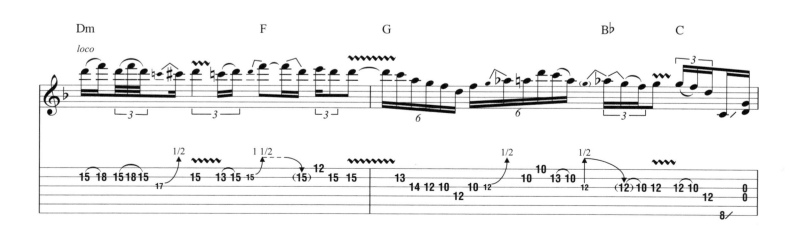

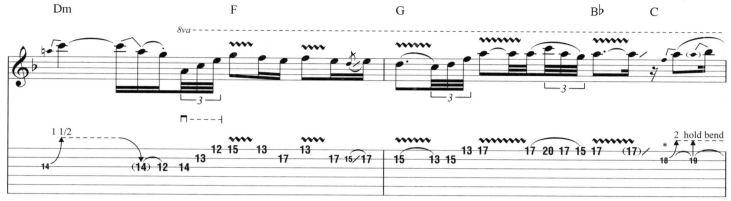

*Bend w/ ring finger, then slur w/ pinky.

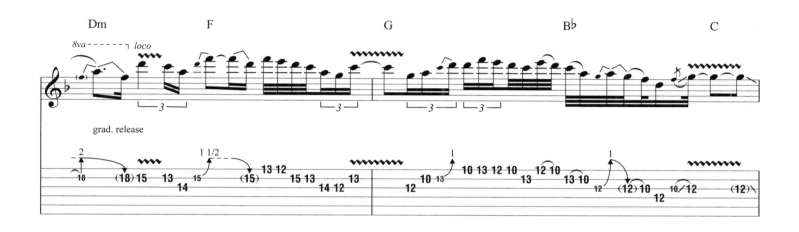

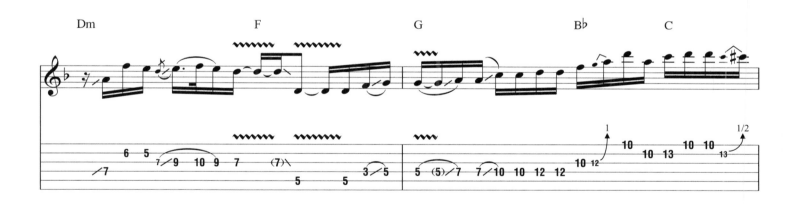

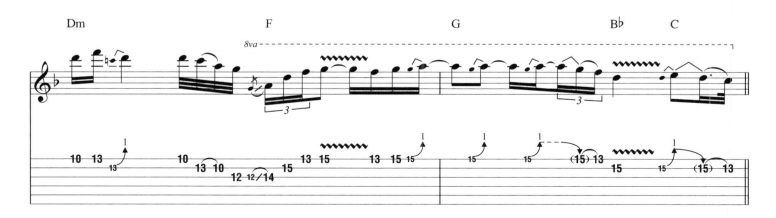

I hate to go home __ a - lone, __ but what else __ is new?

loco

let ring - - - - - - - - - -

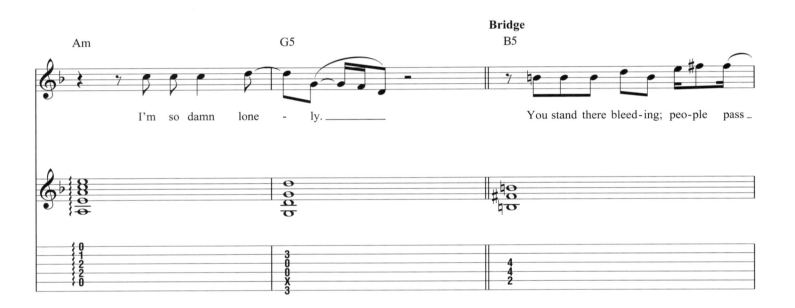

I'm so damn lone - ly. __

Bridge

You stand there bleed-ing; peo-ple pass __

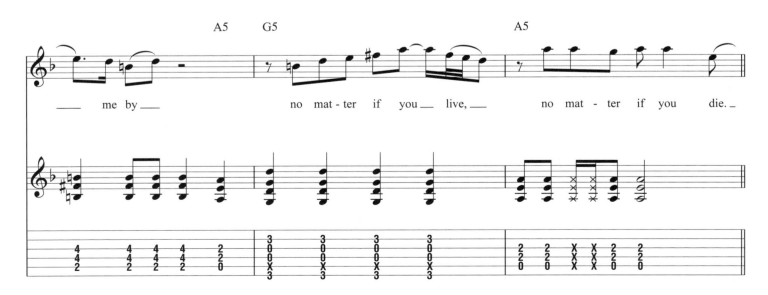

__ me by __ no mat - ter if you __ live, __ no mat - ter if you die. __

Verse

Gtr. tacet

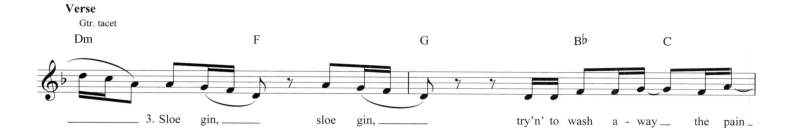

3. Sloe gin, sloe gin, try'n' to wash a - way the pain

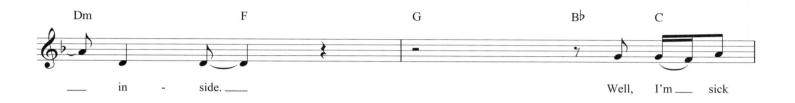

in - side. Well, I'm sick

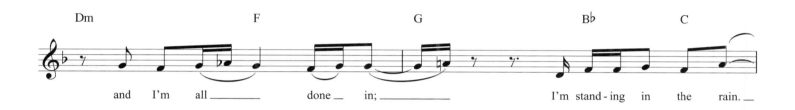

and I'm all done in; I'm stand - ing in the rain.

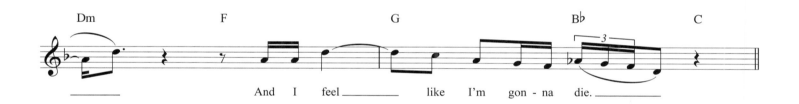

And I feel like I'm gon - na die.

Chorus

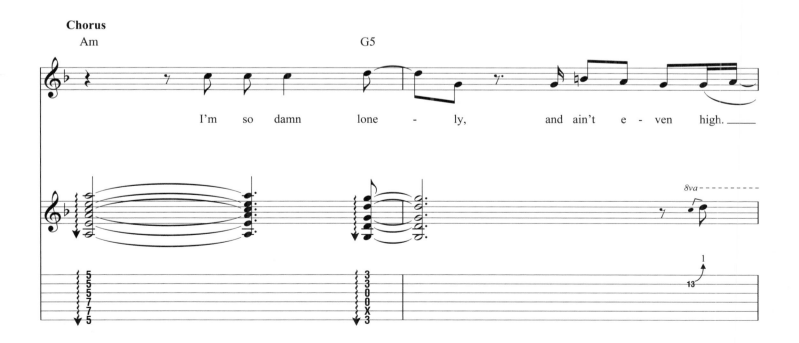

I'm so damn lone - ly, and ain't e - ven high.

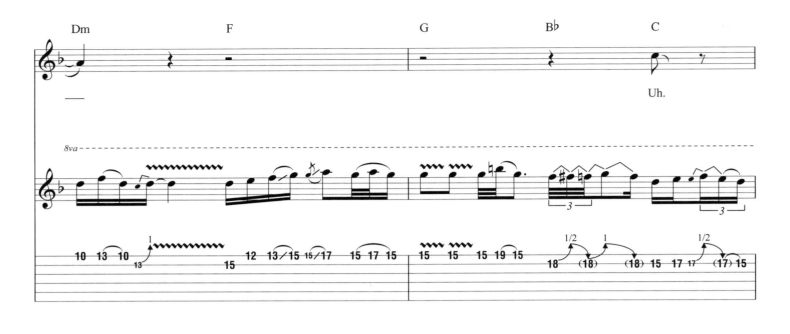

w/ sirens

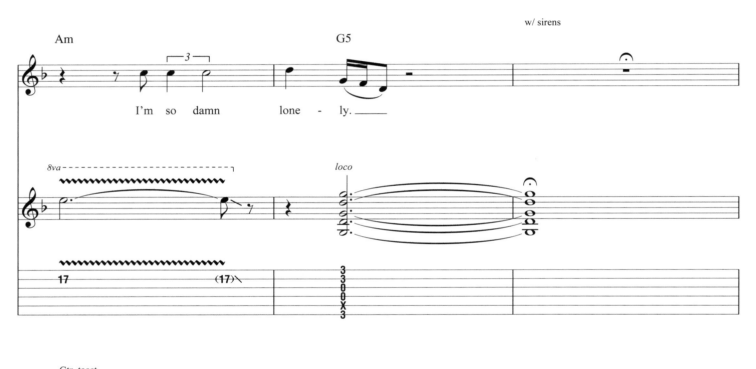

I'm so damn lone - ly. ___

Gtr. tacet

Outro-Guitar Solo

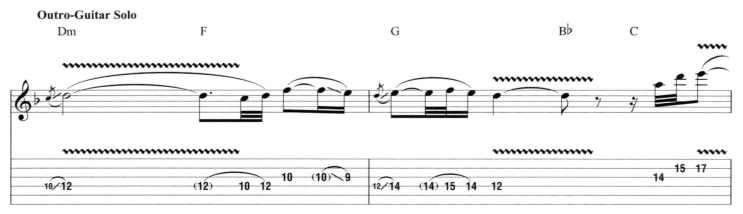

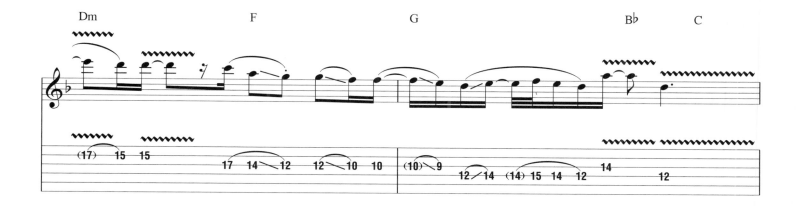

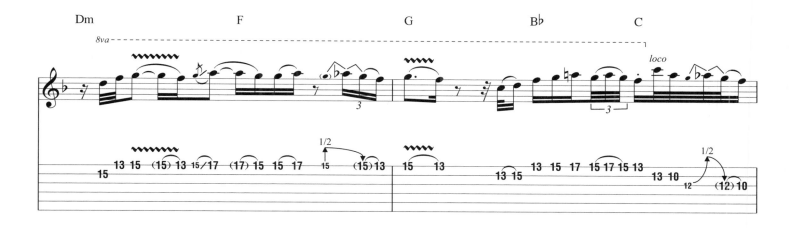

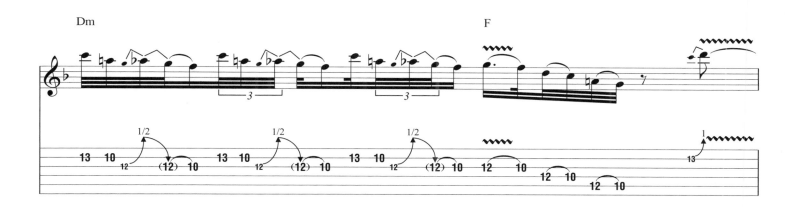

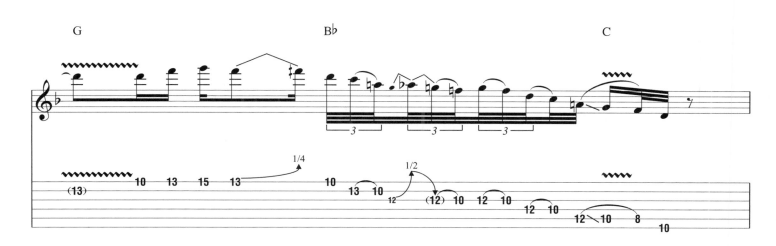

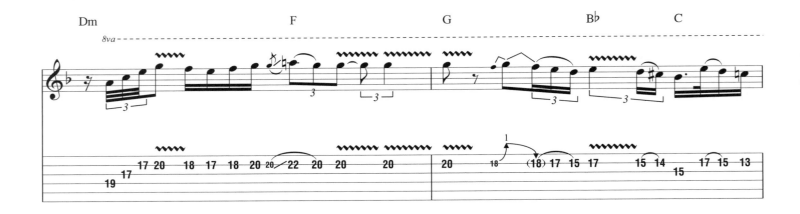

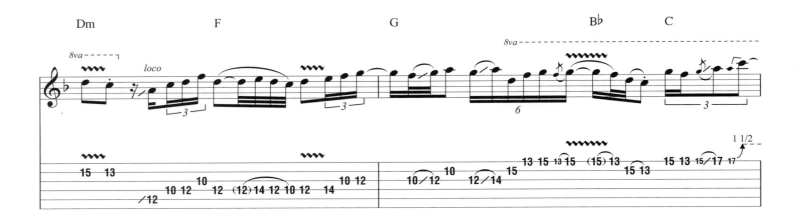

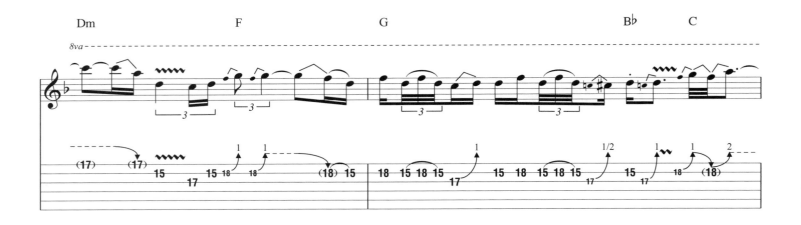

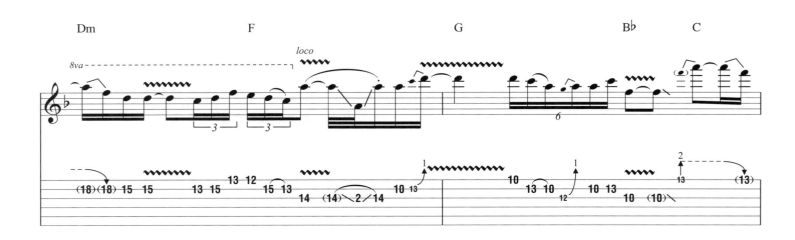

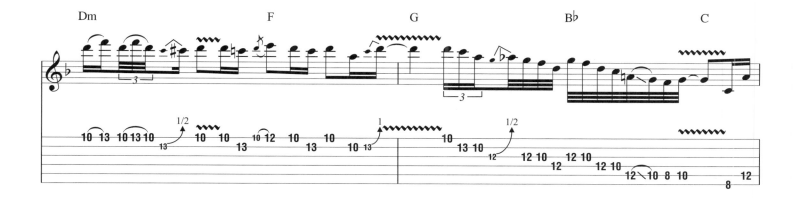

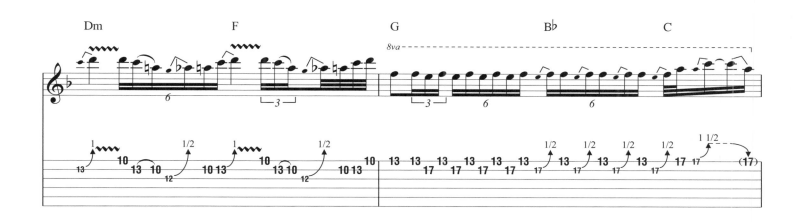

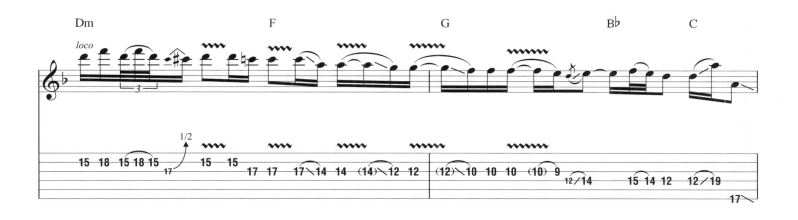

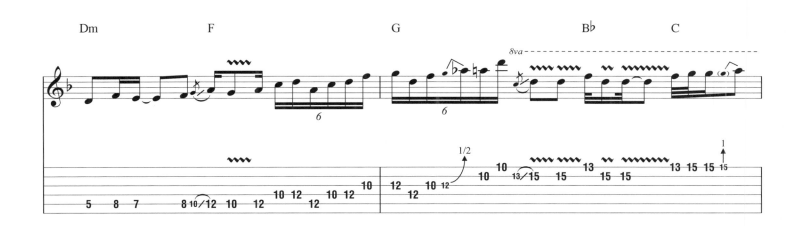

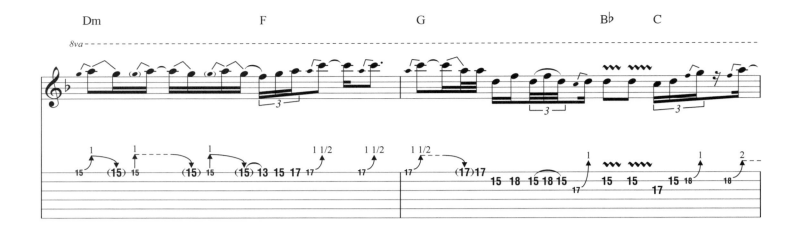

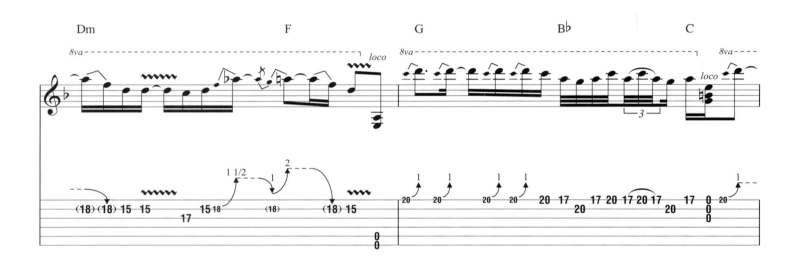

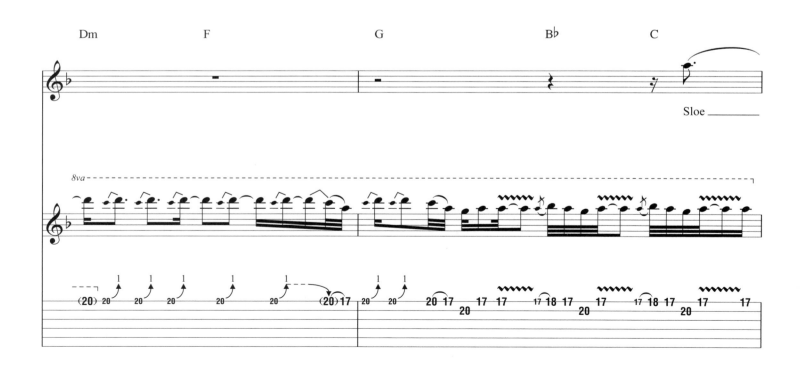

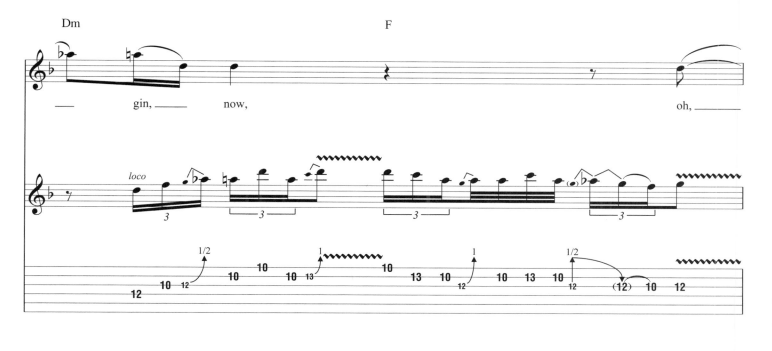

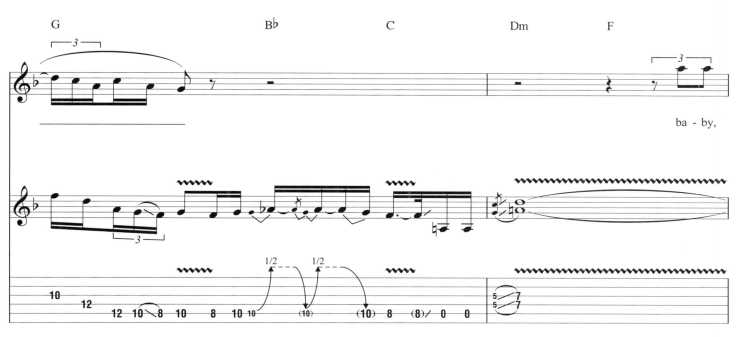

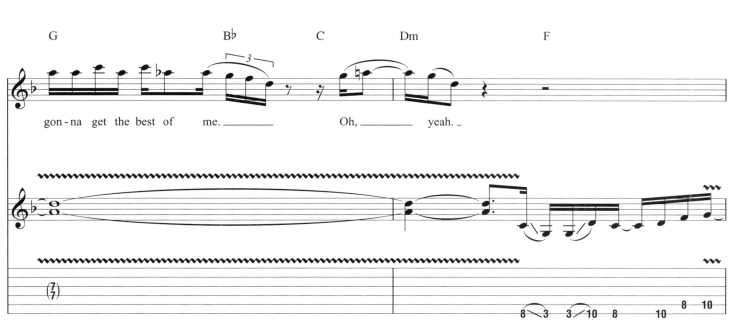

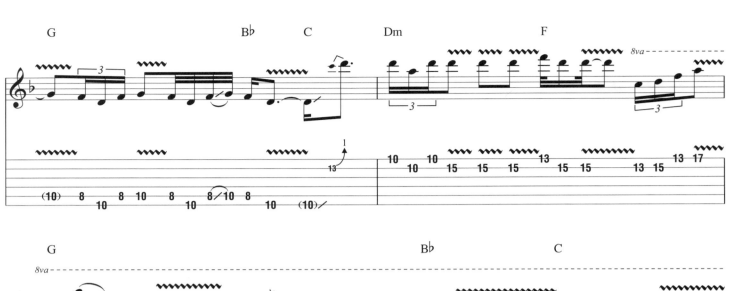

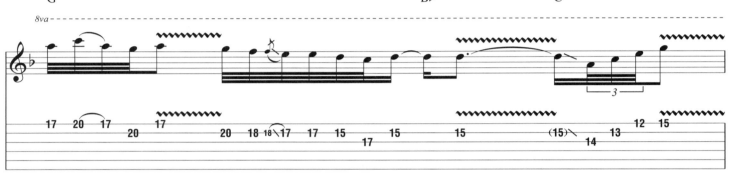

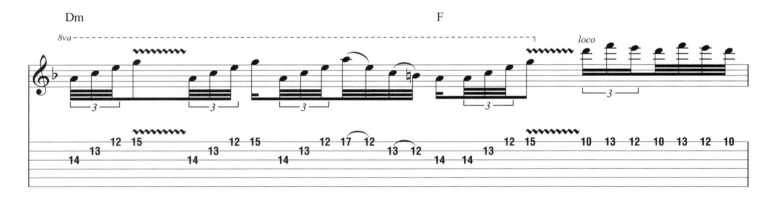

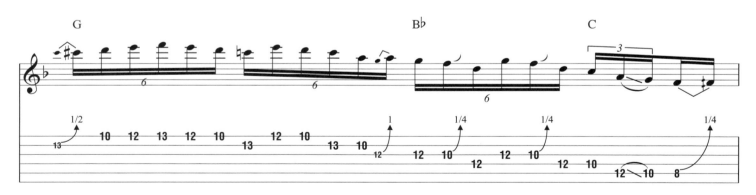

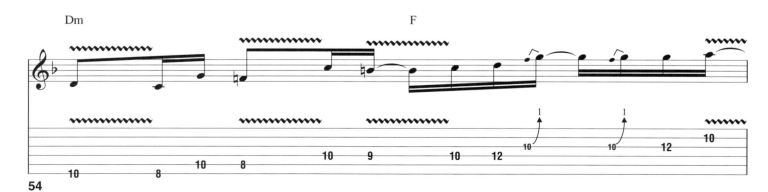

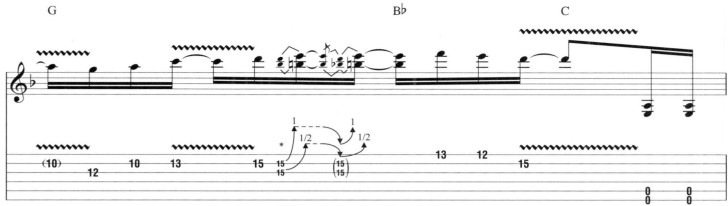

*Allow 3rd string to be caught under ring finger.

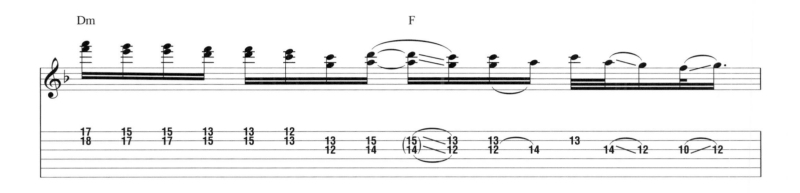

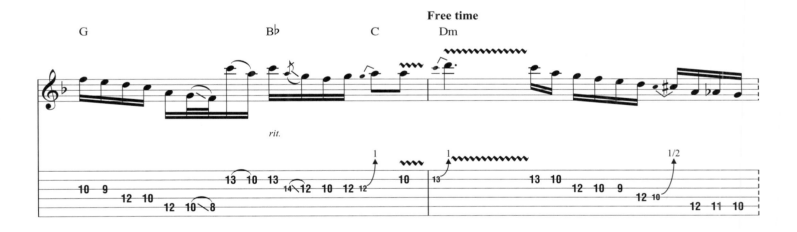

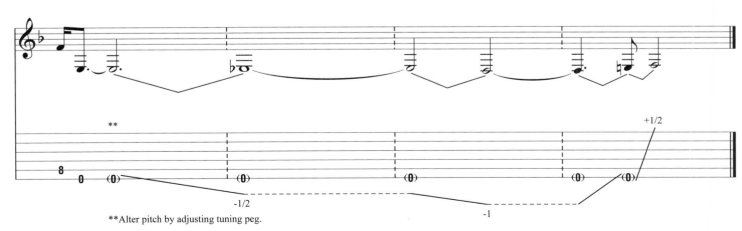

**Alter pitch by adjusting tuning peg.

Last Kiss

Words and Music by Joe Bonamassa

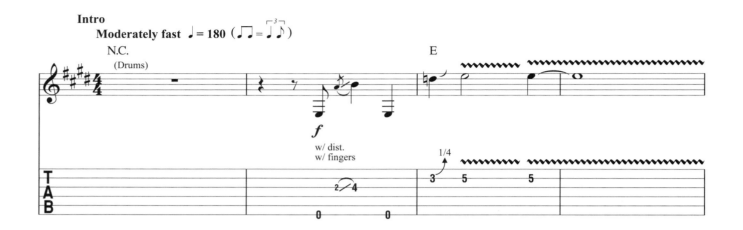

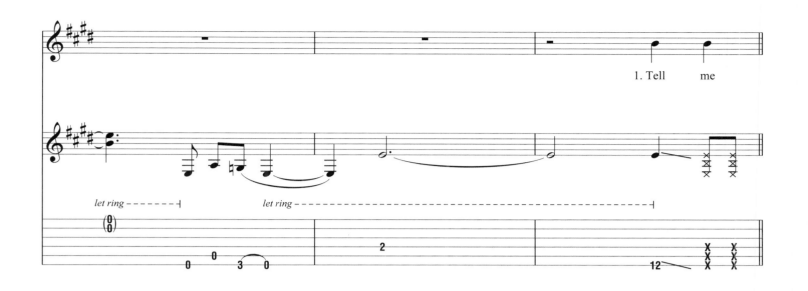

Verse

E

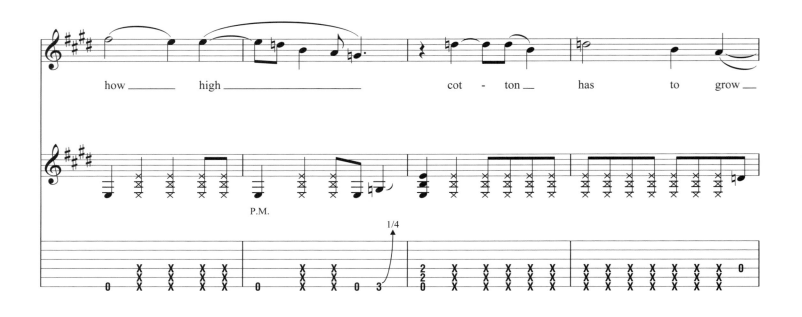

how _____ high _____ cot - ton ___ has to grow ___

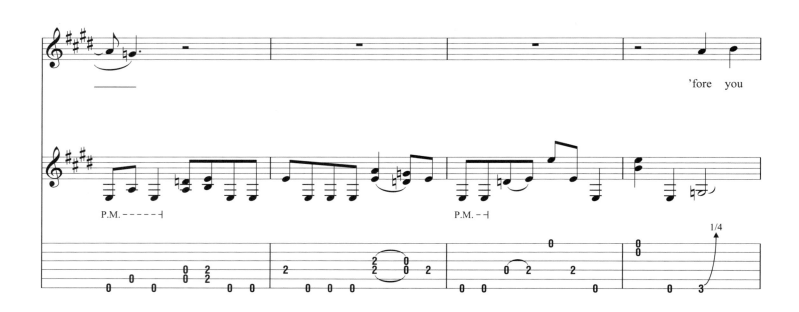

_____ 'fore you

get a man _____ with __ a rust - y blade and a hoe. __

Verse

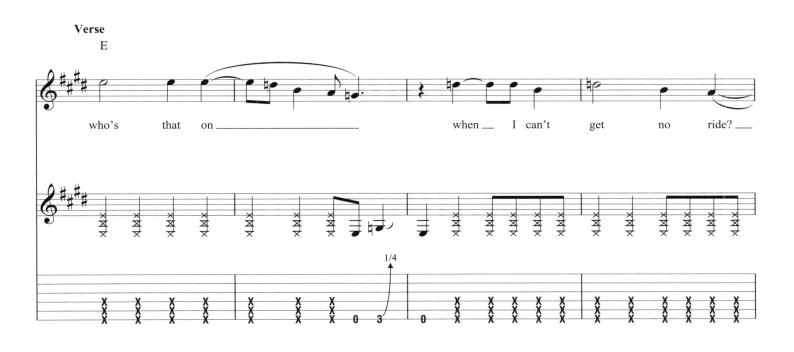

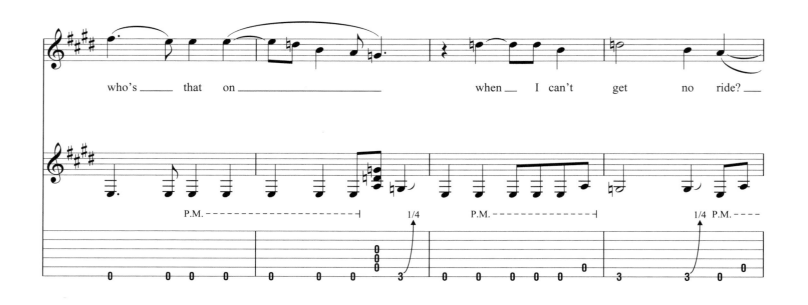

who's ___ that on _____ when ___ I can't get no ride? ___

_____ That's why

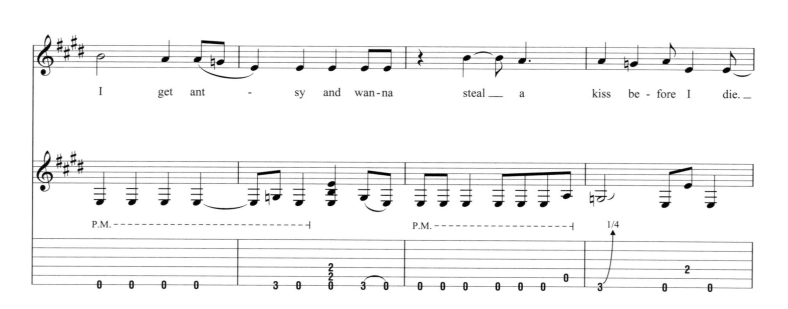

I get ant - sy and wan-na steal ___ a kiss be-fore I die. ___

60

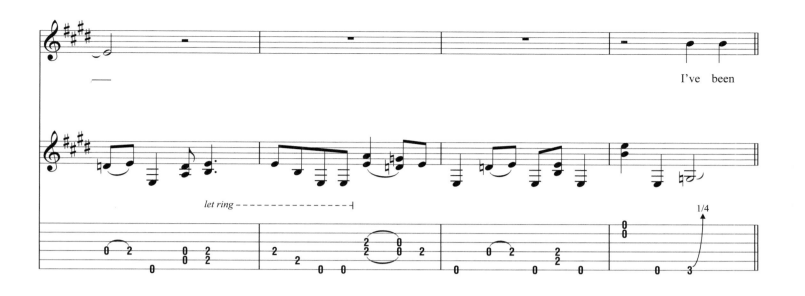

I've been

Chorus

E

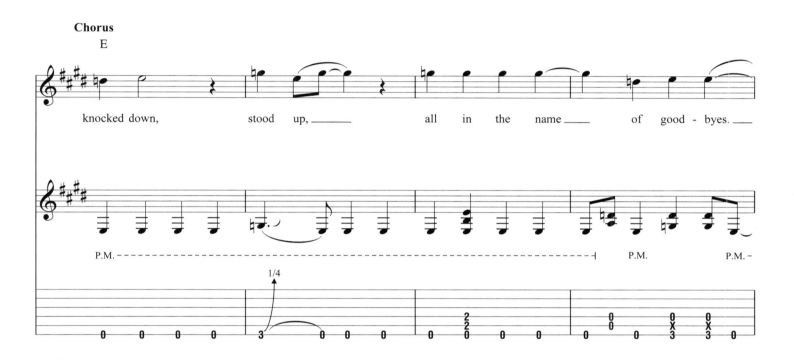

knocked down,   stood up, _____   all   in   the   name ___ of   good - byes. ___

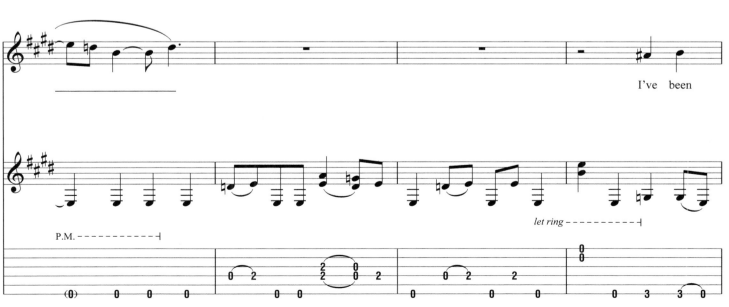

I've been

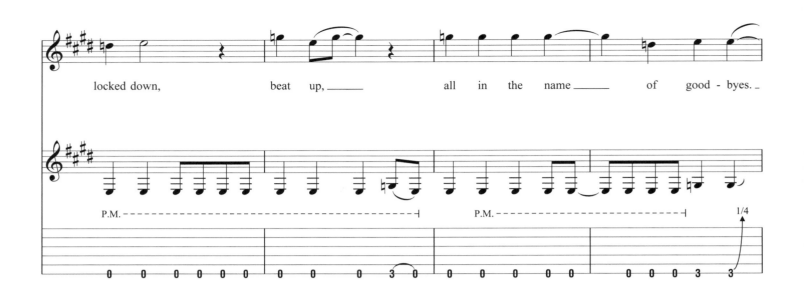

locked down, beat up, _____ all in the name _____ of good - byes. _____

_____ Mm. _____ And I

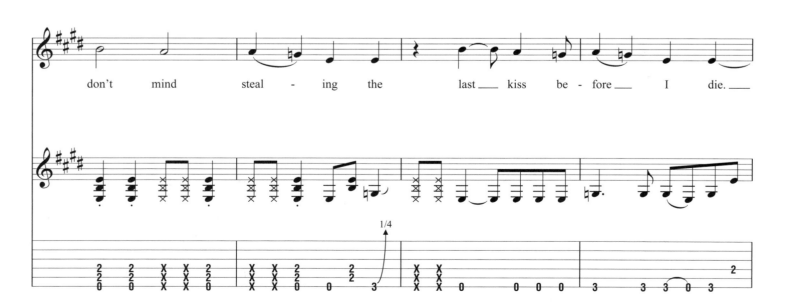

don't mind steal - ing the last _____ kiss be - fore _____ I die. _____

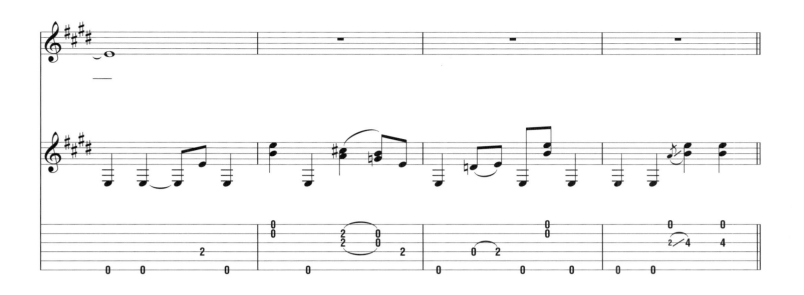

Interlude

E

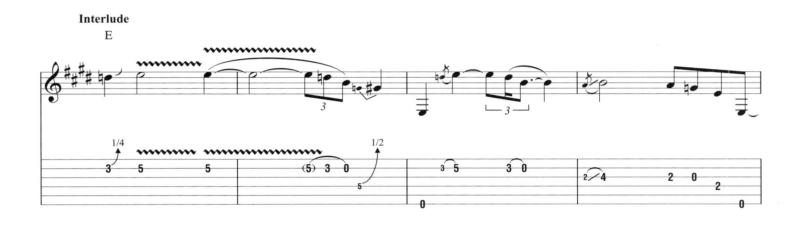

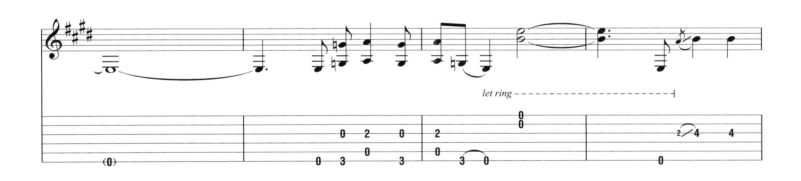

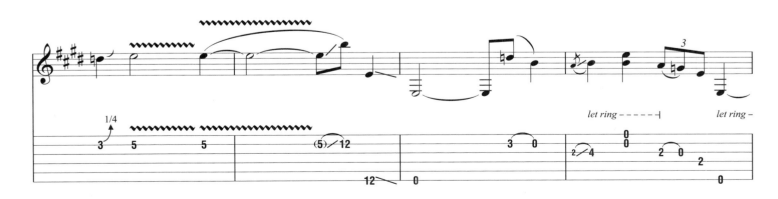

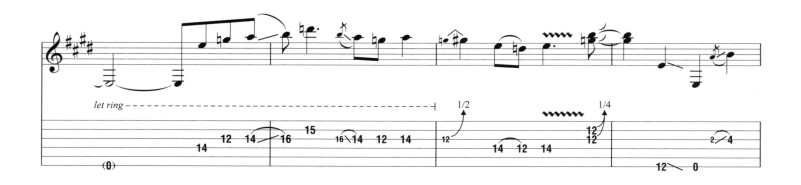

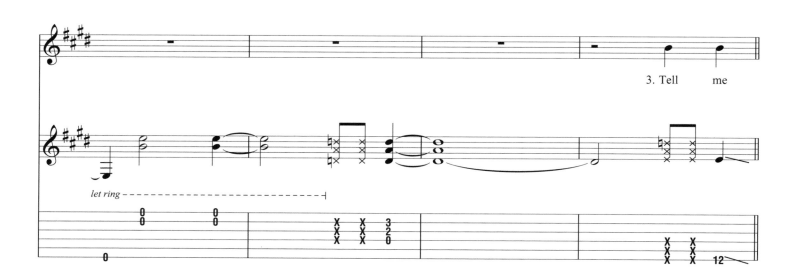

3. Tell me

Verse

E

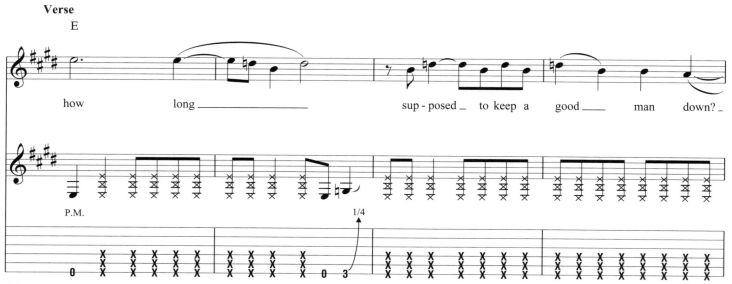

how   long _____   sup - posed _ to keep a   good ____ man   down? _

P.M.

64

Tell me

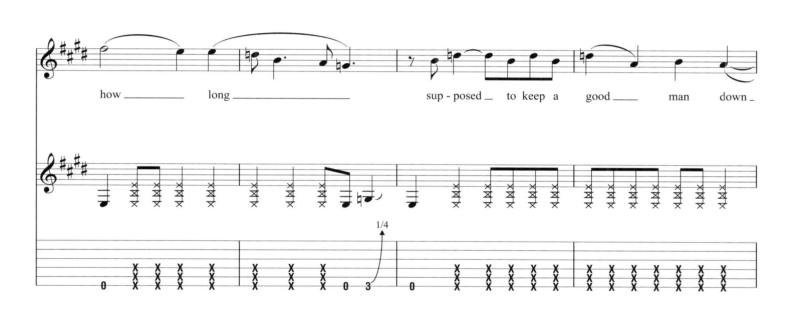

how _____ long _____ sup - posed ___ to keep a good _____ man down _

_____ 'fore he

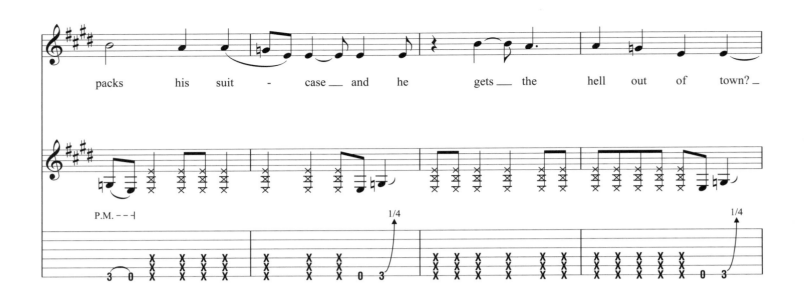

packs his suit - case __ and he gets __ the hell out of town? __

__ 4. Now that

Verse

E

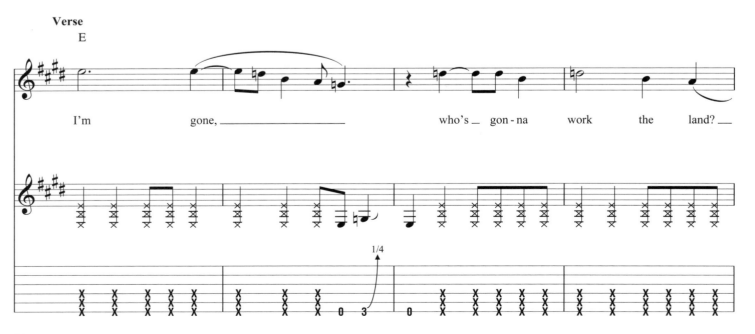

I'm gone, _____ who's __ gon - na work the land? __

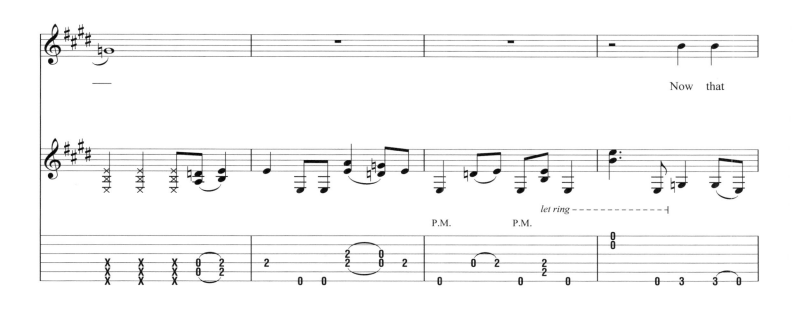

Now that

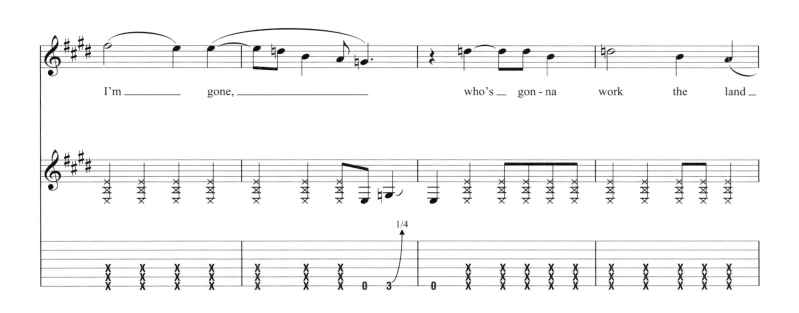

I'm ___ gone, ___ who's ___ gon - na work the land ___

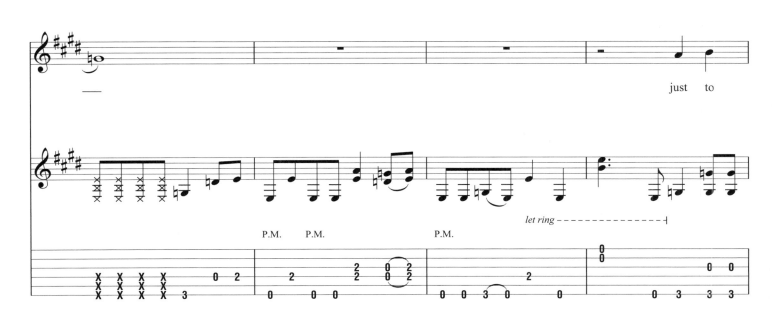

just to

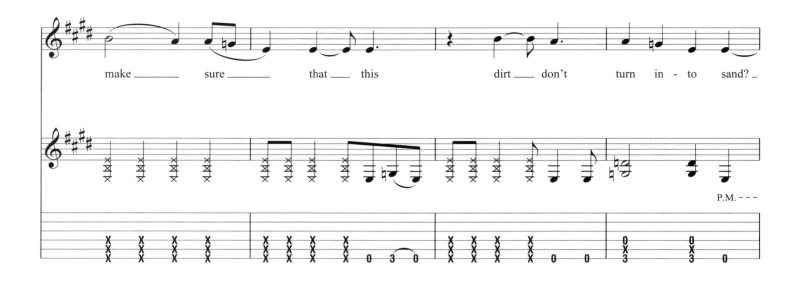

make _____ sure _____ that _____ this _____ dirt _____ don't turn in - to sand? _

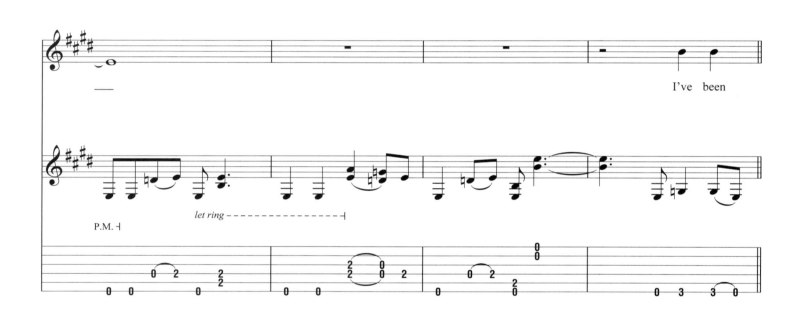

— I've been

𝄋 Chorus

E

knocked down, _____ stood up, _____ all in the name _____ of good - byes. _____

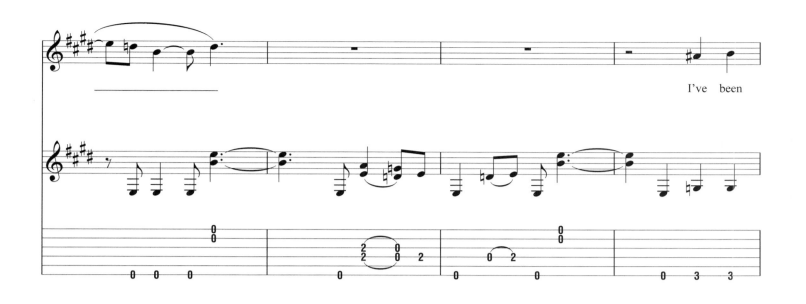

locked down, beat up, _____ all in the name _____ of good - byes. _____

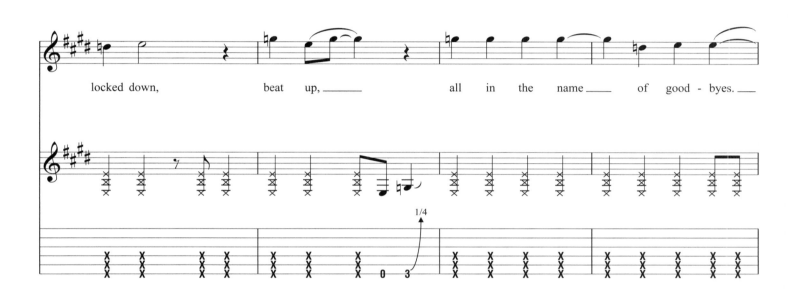

Mm. _____ And I

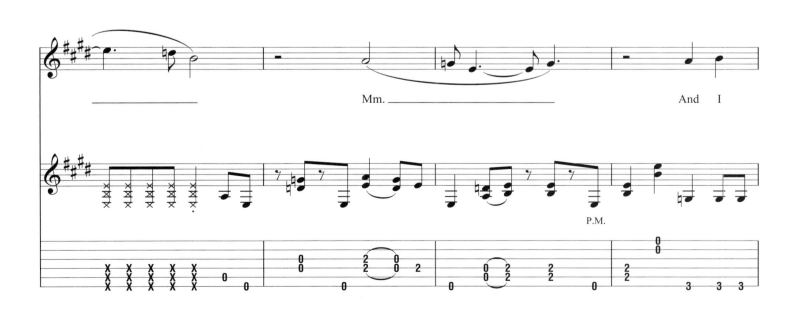

P.M.

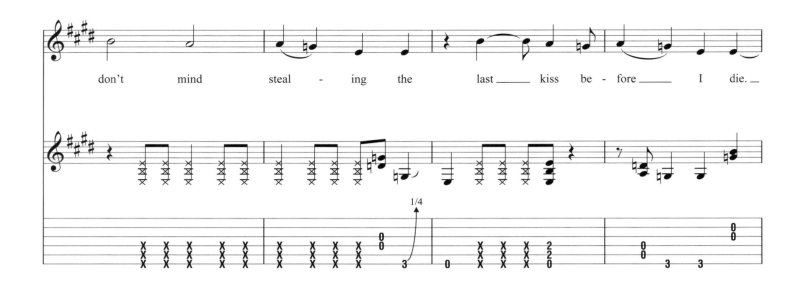

don't mind steal - ing the last ____ kiss be - fore ____ I die. ____

To Coda ⊕

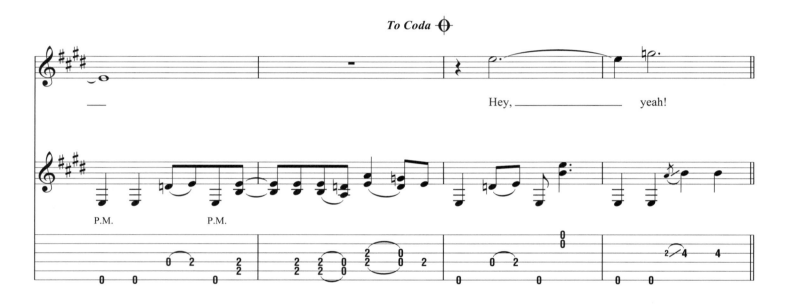

Hey, _____ yeah!

Interlude

E

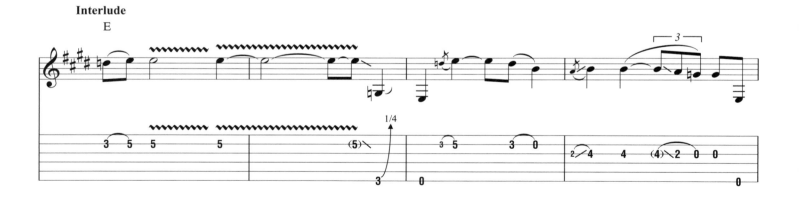

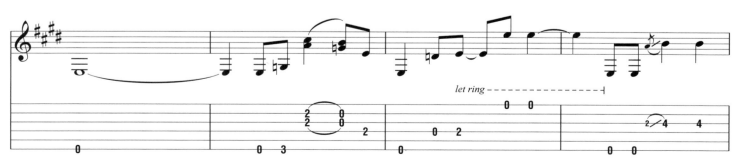

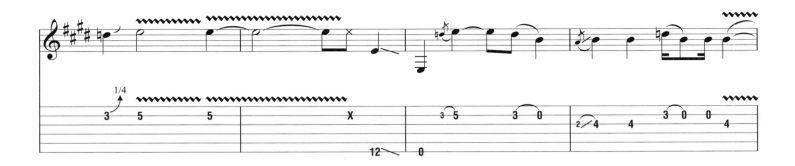

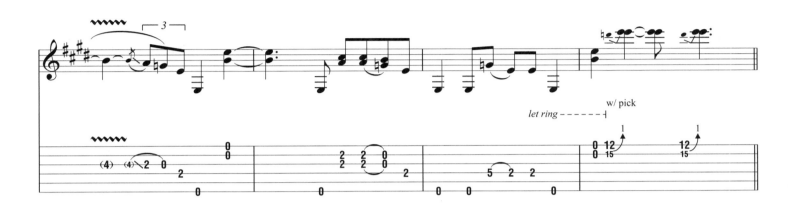

Guitar Solo

E

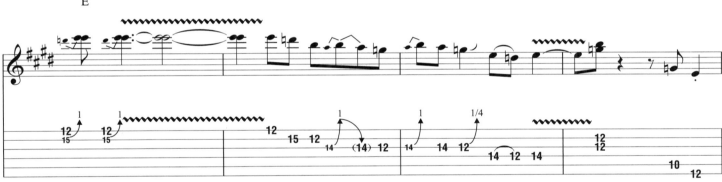

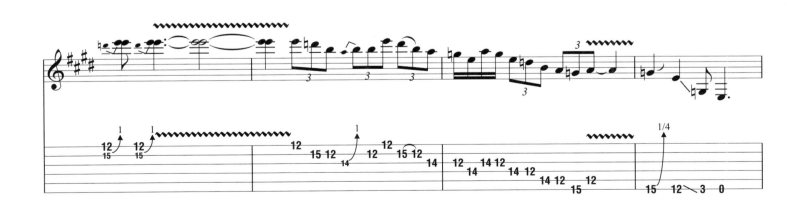

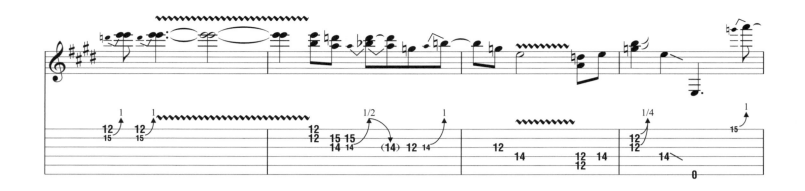

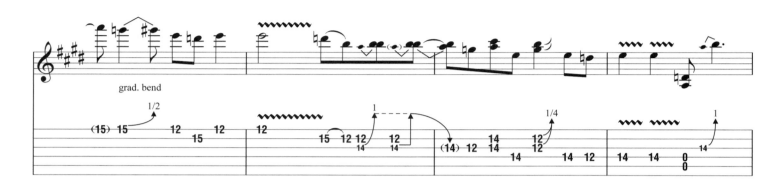

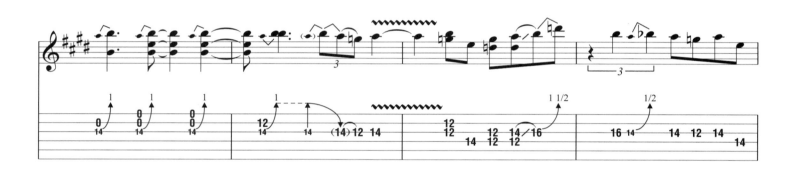

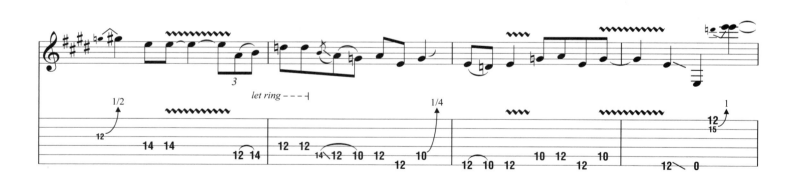

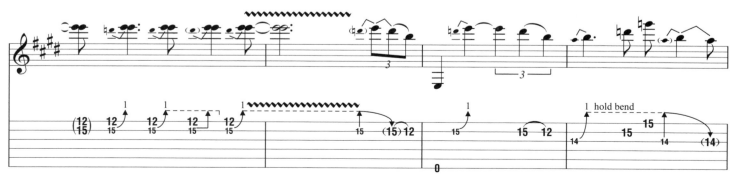

I've been

⊕ Coda

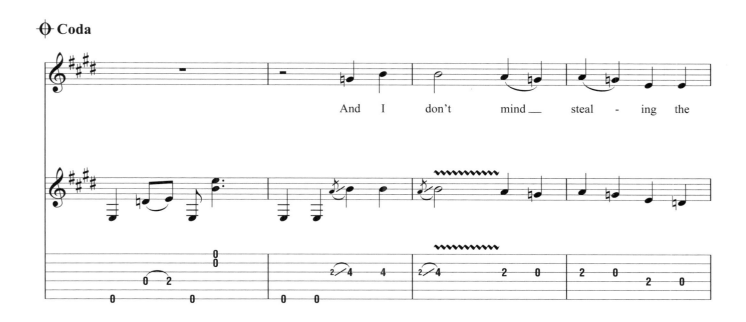

And I don't mind ___ steal - ing the

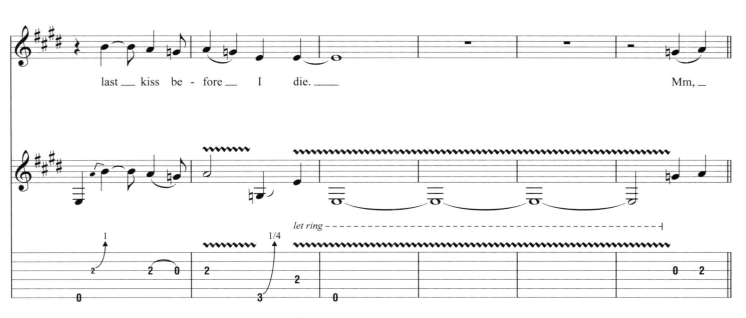

last ___ kiss be - fore ___ I die. ___ Mm, ___

Outro

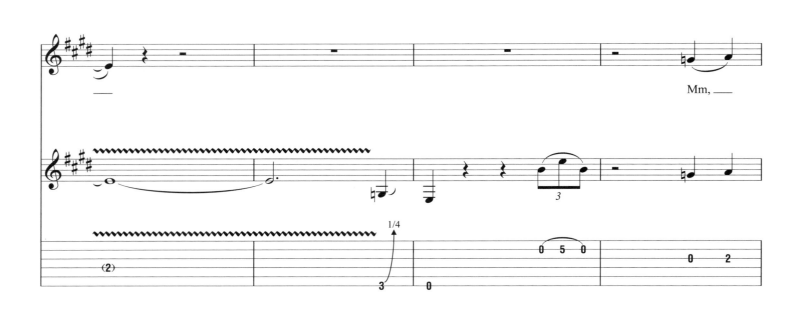

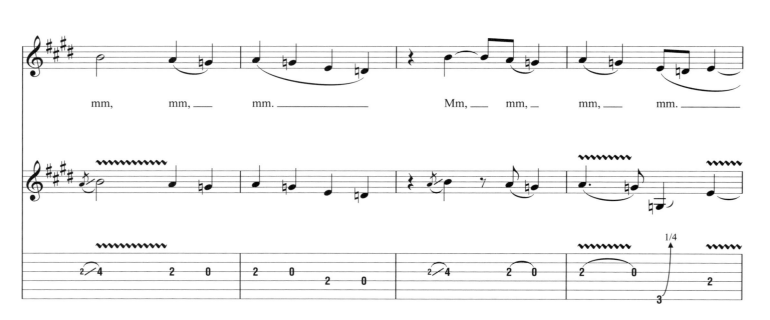

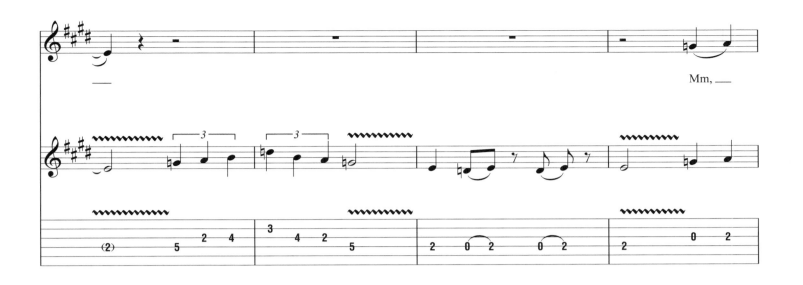

Mm, ___

mm, ___ mm, ___ mm. ___ Mm, ___ mm, ___ mm, ___ mm. ___

Mm, ___

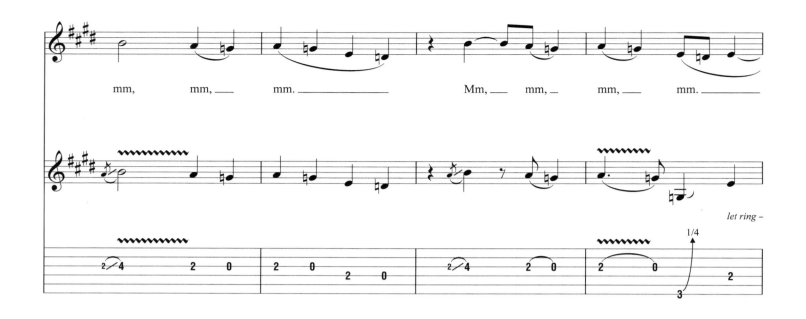

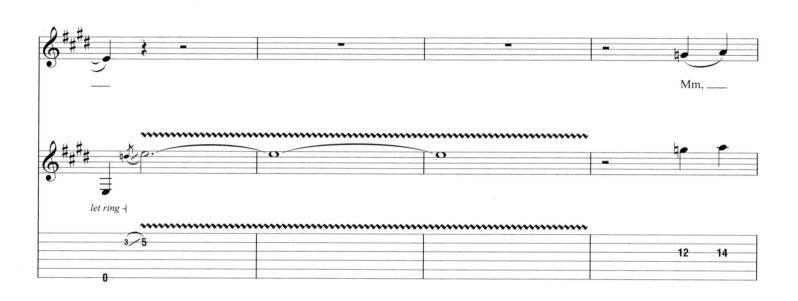

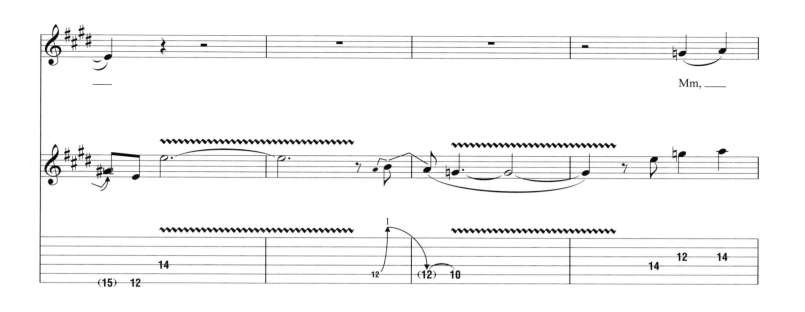

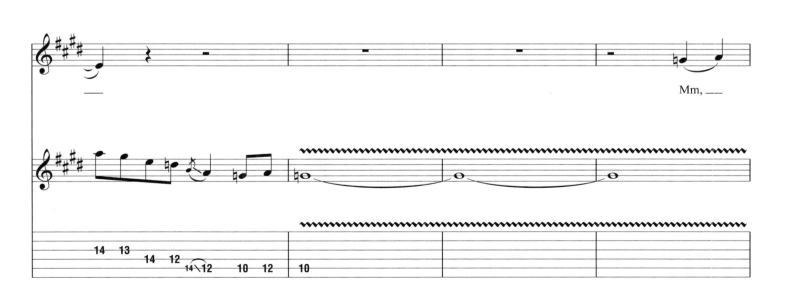

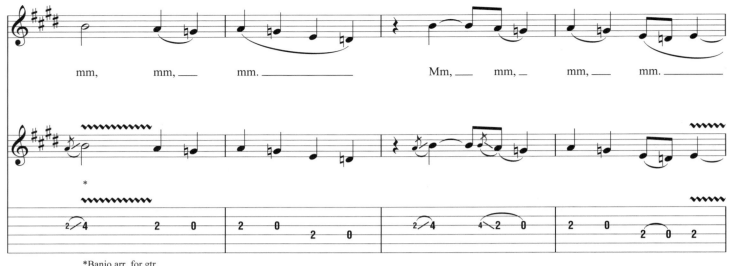

*Banjo arr. for gtr.

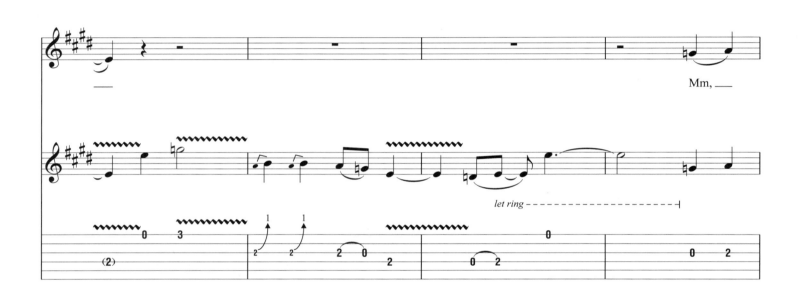

Lonesome Road Blues

Words and Music by Joe Bonamassa

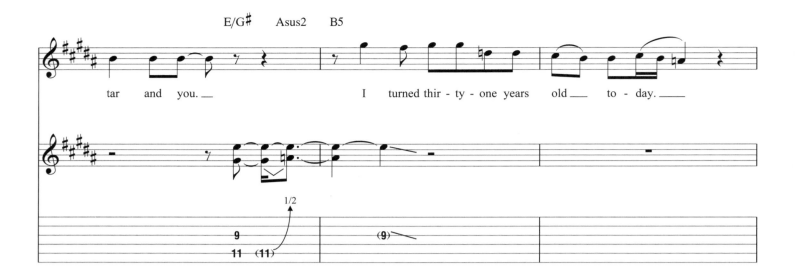

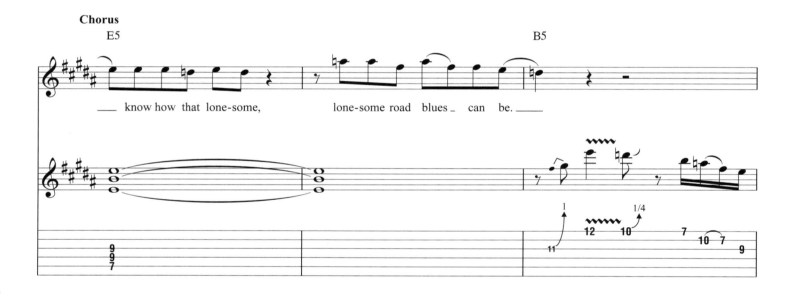

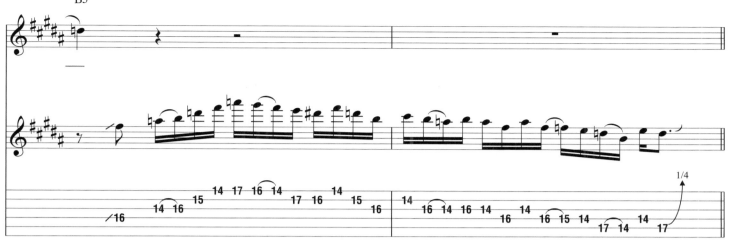

Verse

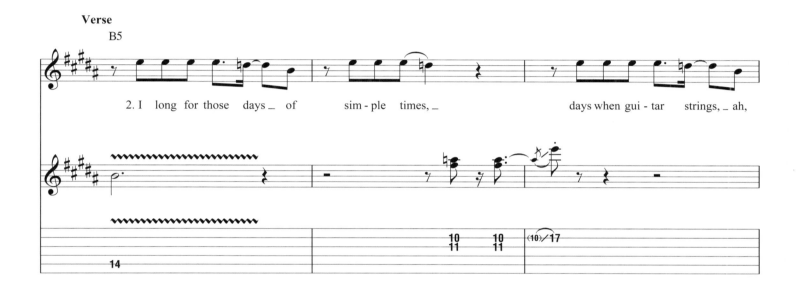

2. I long for those days __ of sim - ple times, __   days when gui - tar strings, __ ah,

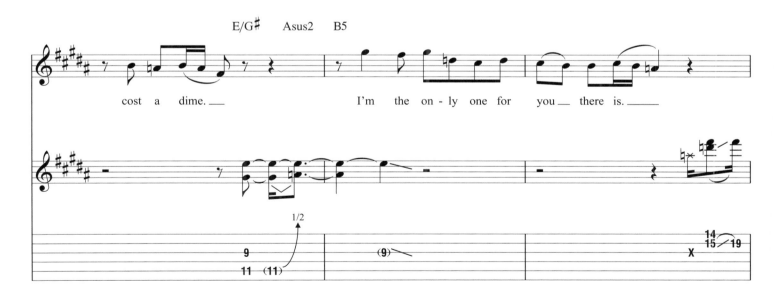

cost a dime. __   I'm the on - ly one for you __ there is. _____

Help me down, __ ba — by; _____   hell, that is. _____ And   I

Chorus

know how that lone-some, lone-some road blues can be.

Like a dev-il race car, ba - by, lone-some road com-fort me.

Mm, mm.

Interlude

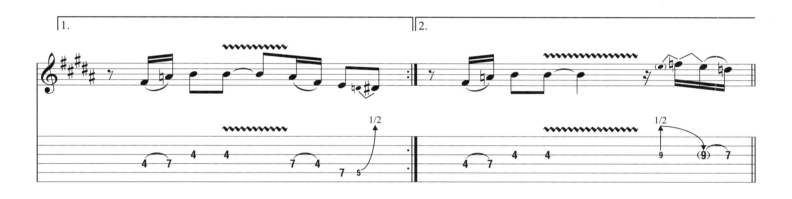

Guitar Solo

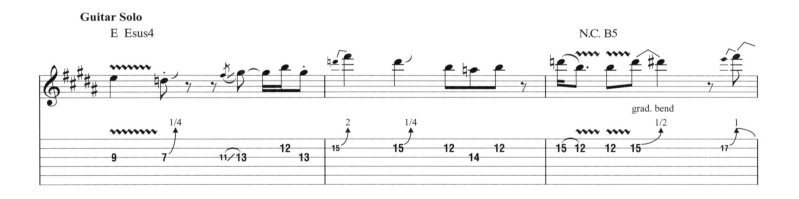

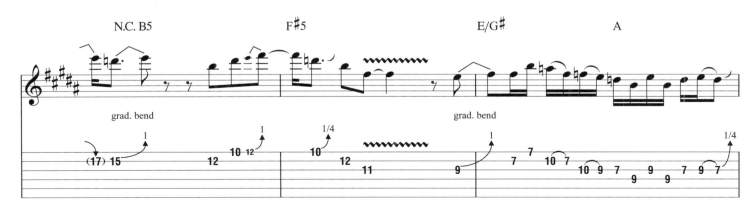

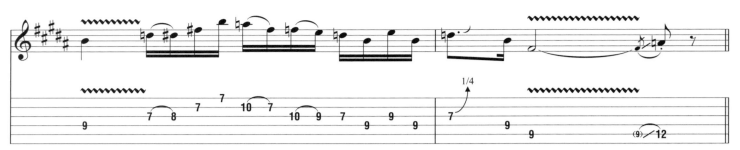

Verse

3. I sold my soul __ for a pack of cig - a - rettes, __ yeah. Mis - sis - sip - pi's where __ I

let ring - - ⌐

think __ my best. __ My __ string is cra - zy; __ I keep her sane. __

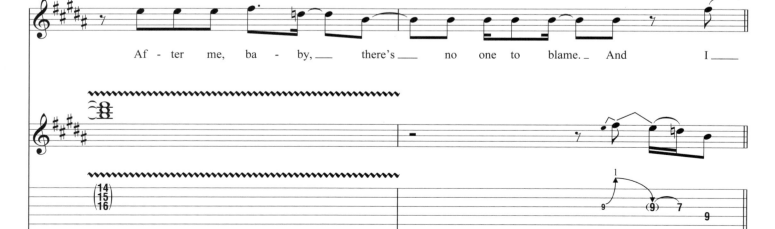

Af - ter me, ba - by, __ there's __ no one to blame. __ And I __

Chorus

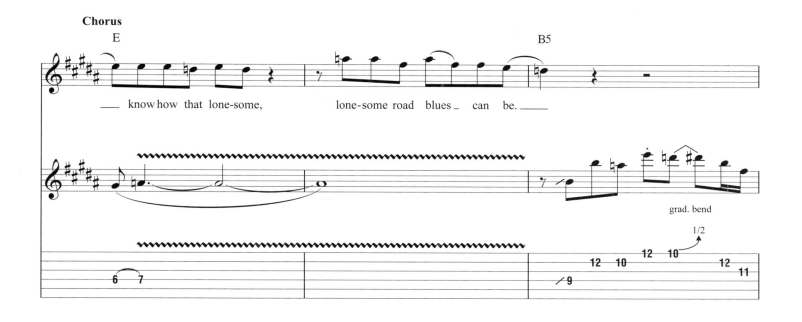

know how that lone-some, lone-some road blues _ can be. _

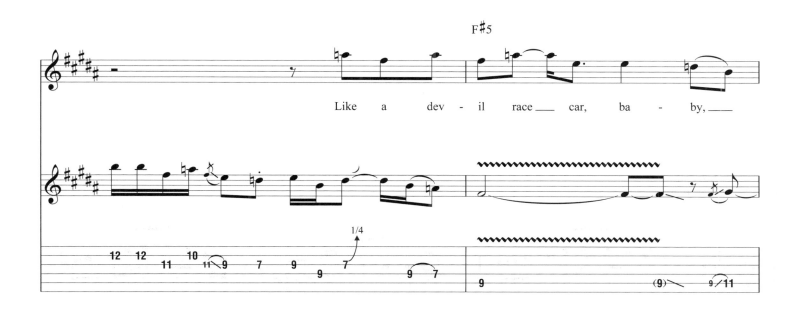

Like a dev - il race _ car, ba - by, _

lone - some road _ com - fort me. _

F#5

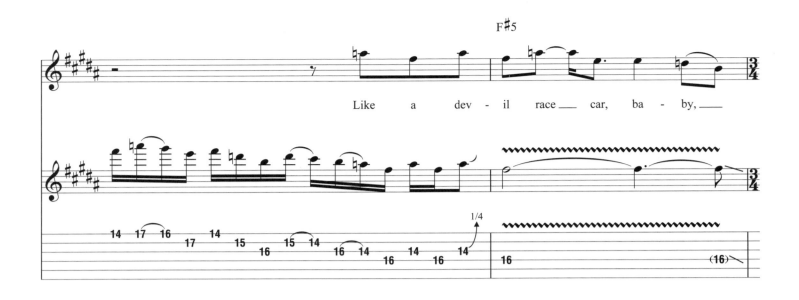

Like a dev - il race car, ba - by, ___

Freely
Gtr. tacet
E/G#

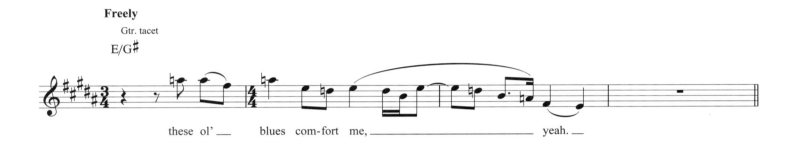

these ol' ___ blues com-fort me, ___ yeah. ___

Interlude
A tempo
B5

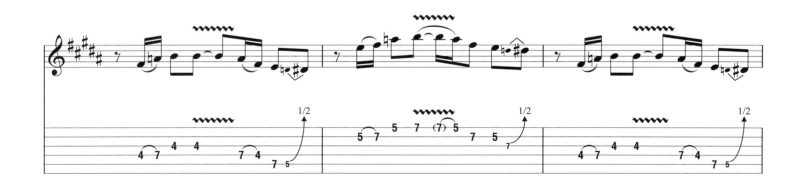

Outro-Guitar Solo

B5

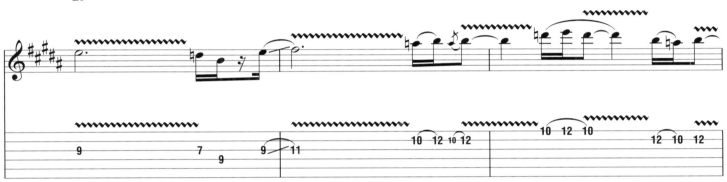

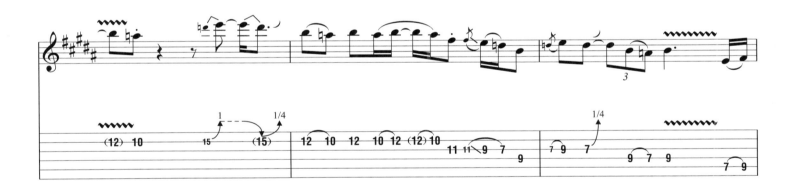

So, It's Like That

Words and Music by Joe Bonamassa and Michael Himelstein

Tune down 1/2 step:
(low to high) 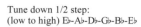 E♭-A♭-D♭-G♭-B♭-E♭

Intro
Moderately ♩ = 130

*Thumb on 6th string throughout where applicable.

1. Well, I was

Verse

Guitar Solo

yeah. _____

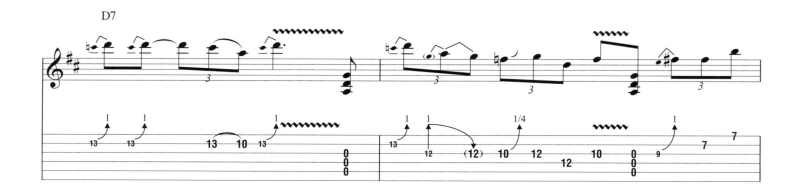

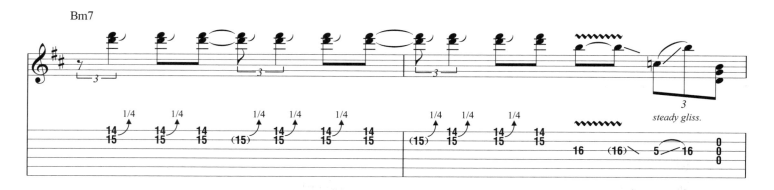

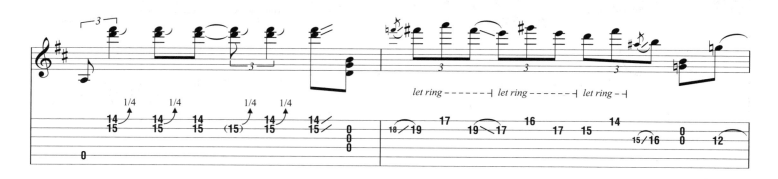

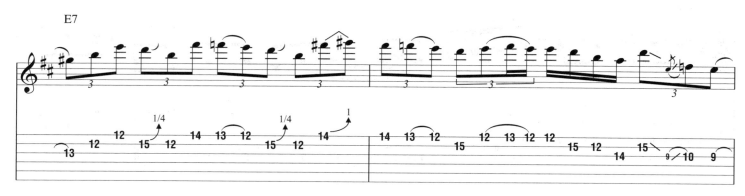

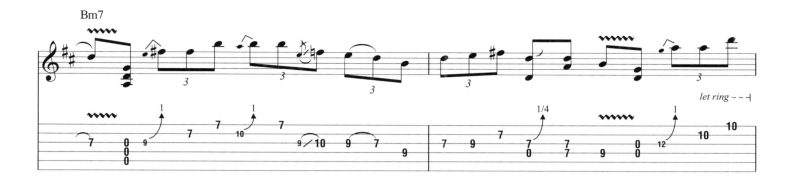

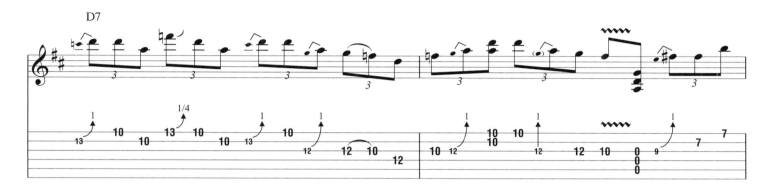

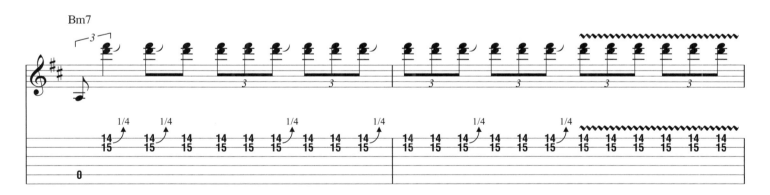

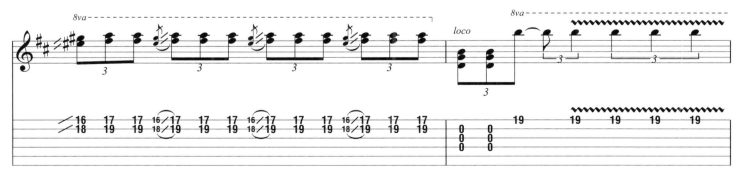

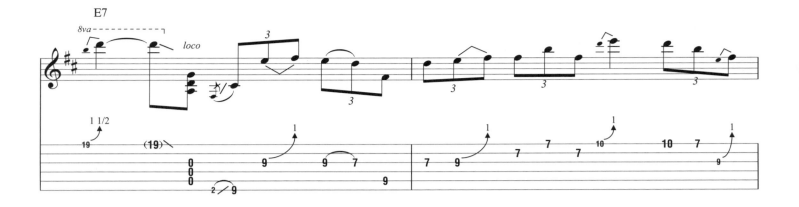

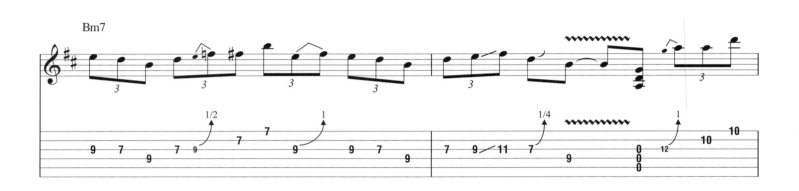

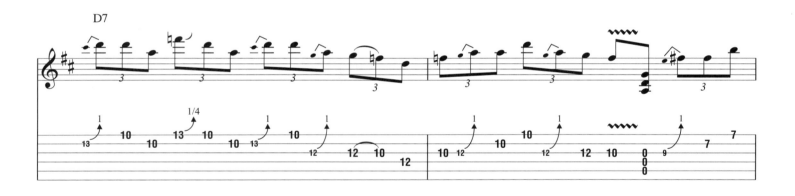

Verse

3. You took my best pos - ses - sion to the

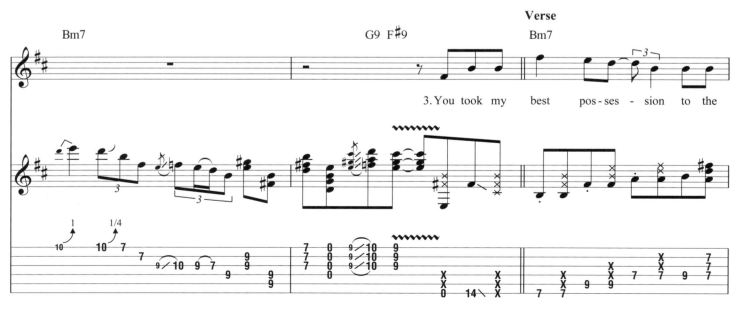

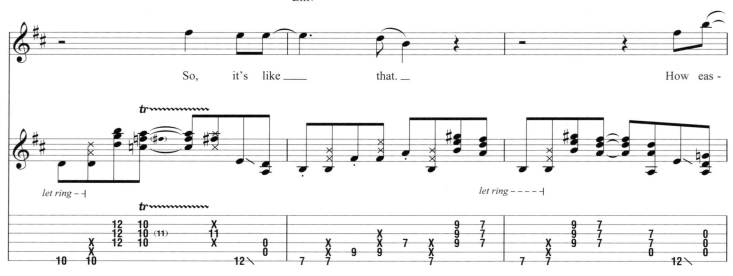

So, it's like ___ that. ___ How eas-

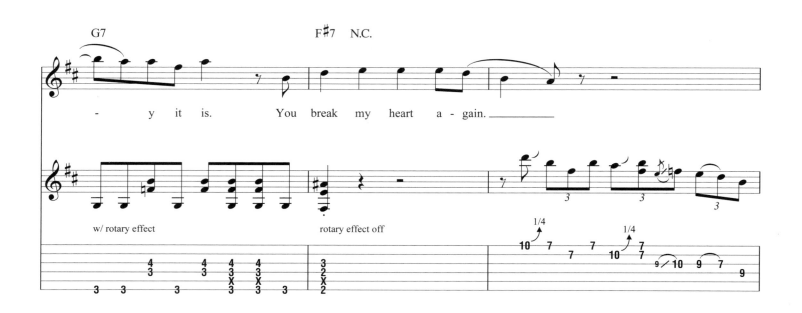

-y it is. You break my heart a-gain. ___

Oh, ___ yeah, ___ yeah. ___

So Many Roads, So Many Trains

Words and Music by Paul Marshall

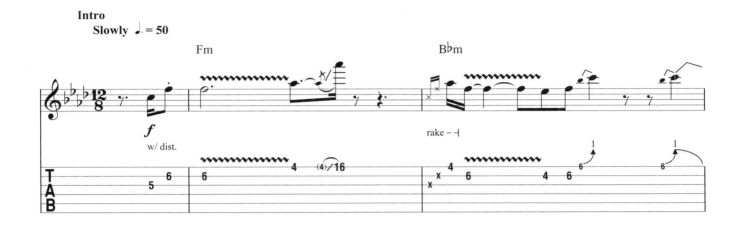

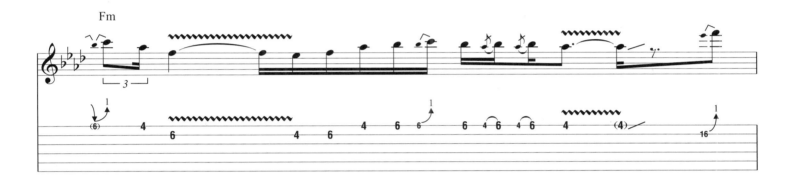

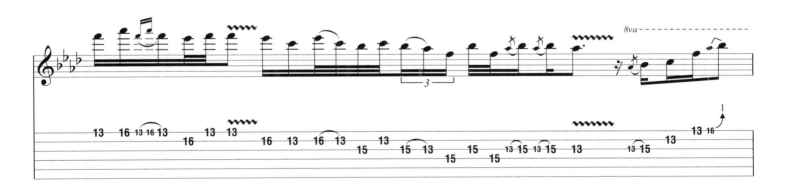

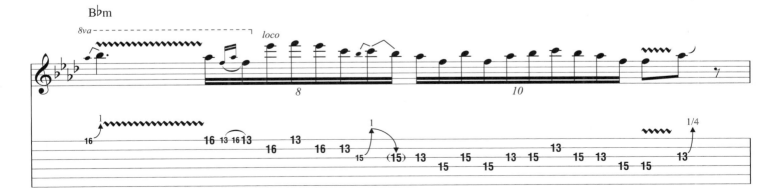

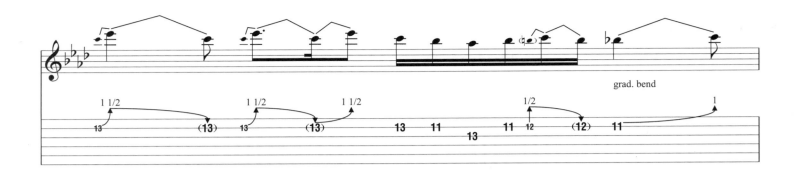

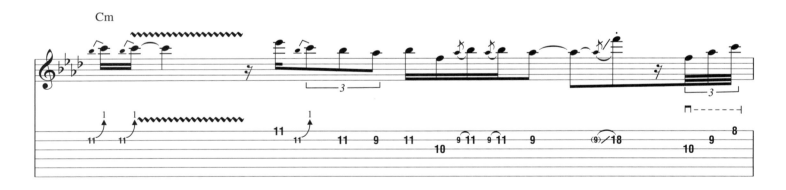

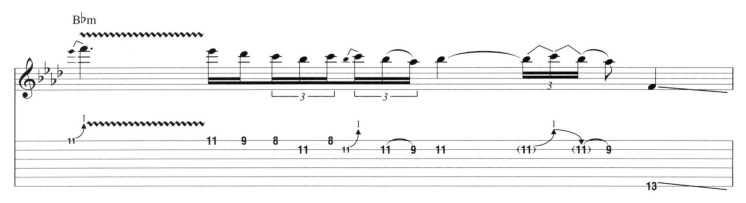

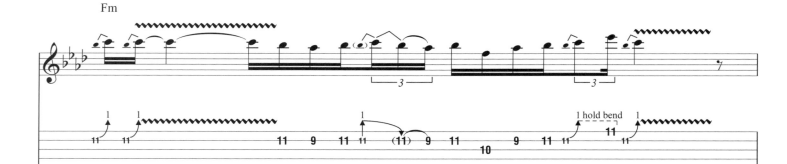

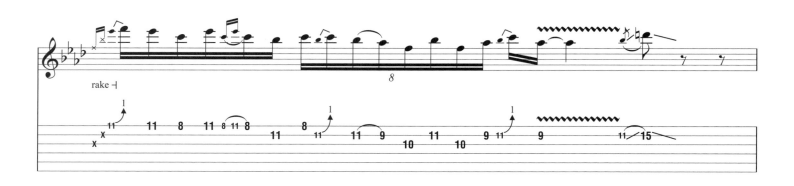

I got to find my ba - by, ___   'fore I _____   can be sat - is - fied. ___

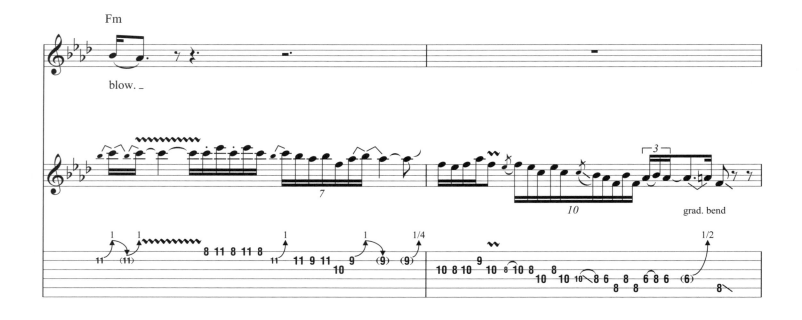

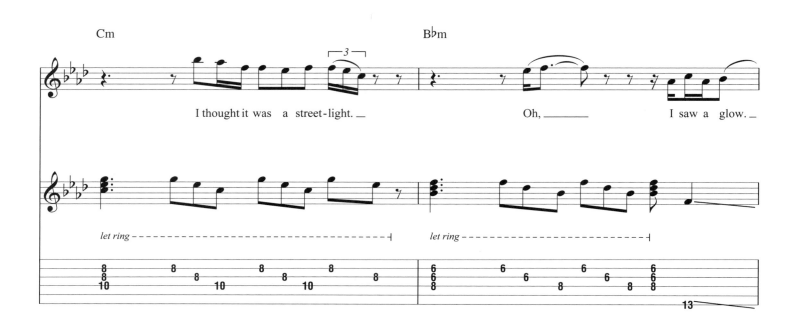

Guitar Solo

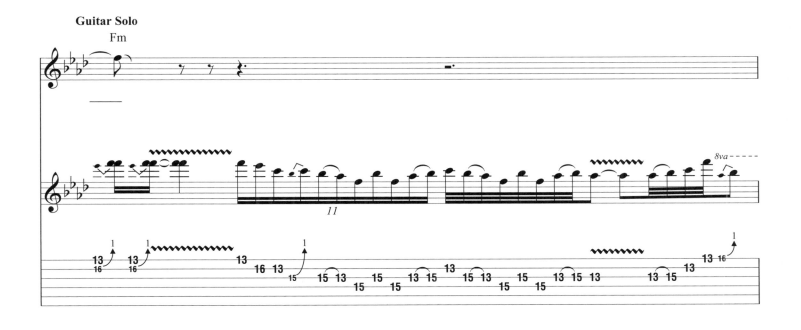

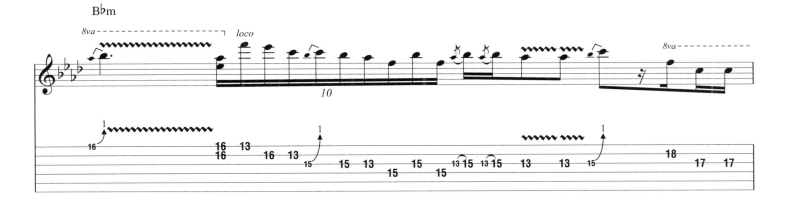

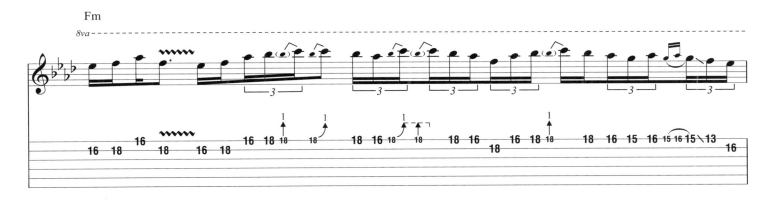

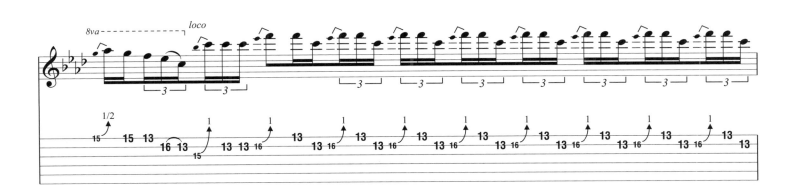

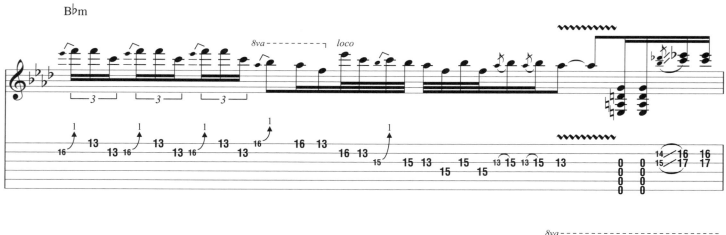

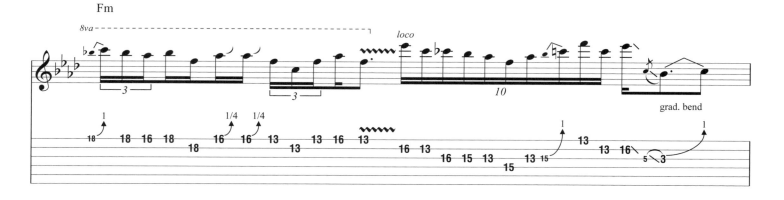

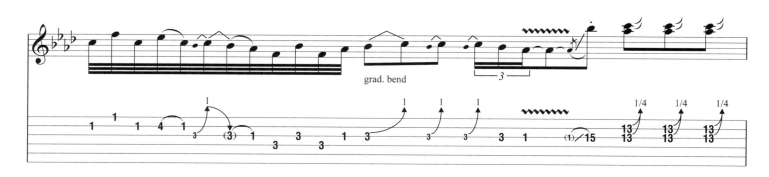

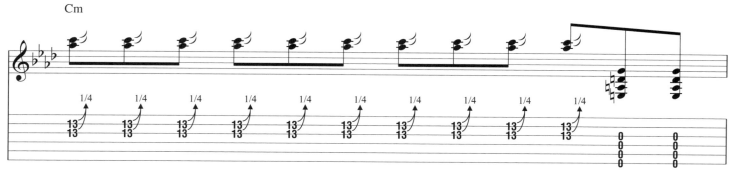

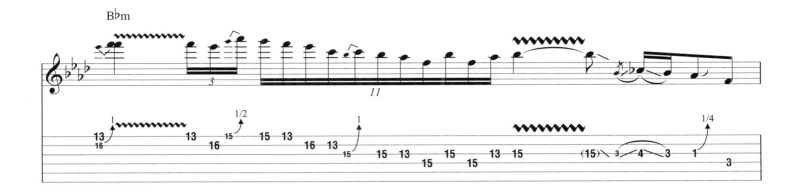

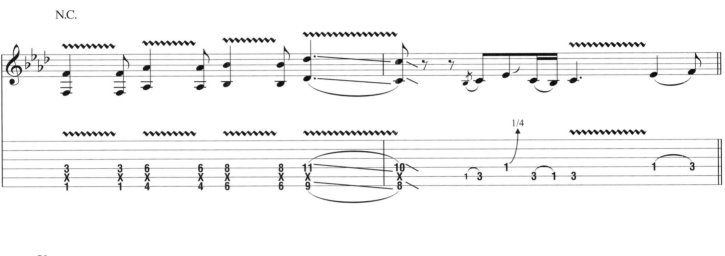

Verse

3. It was a mean old fire-man and a cruel en - gin-eer.

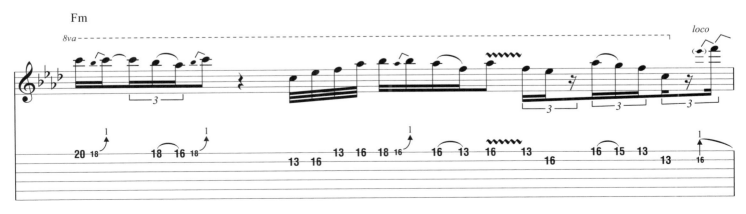

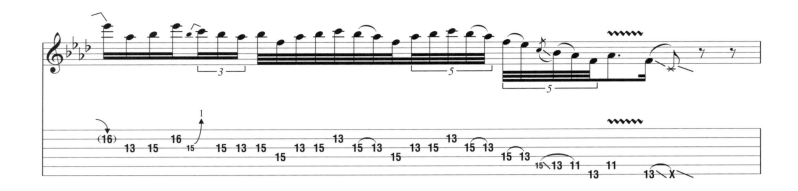

It was a mean _ old fire - man   and a cruel _____ en - gin-eer. _

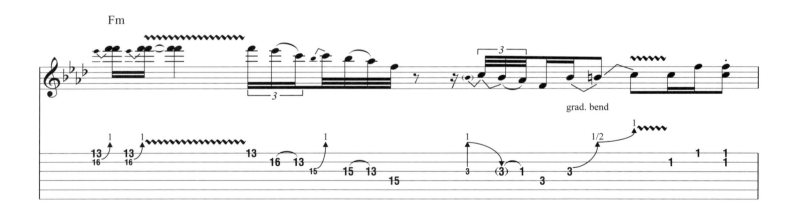

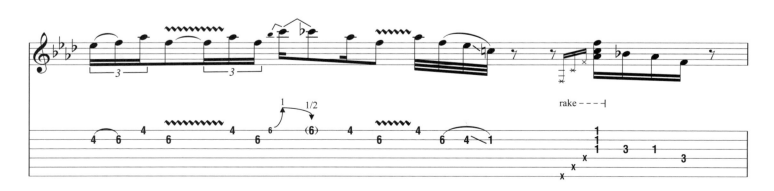

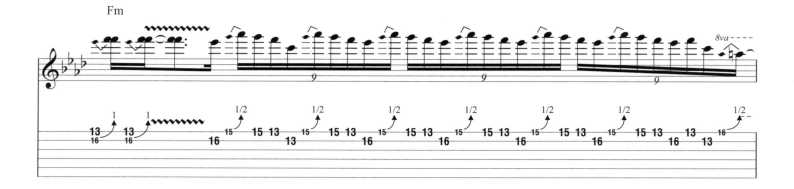

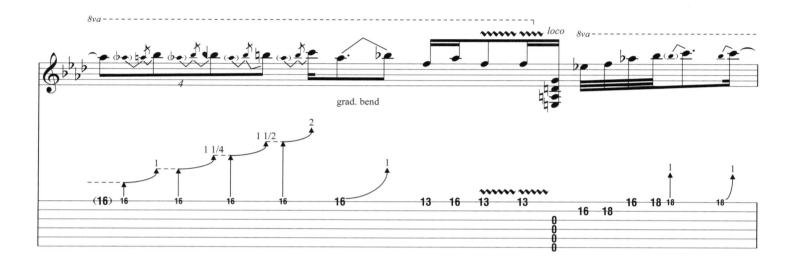

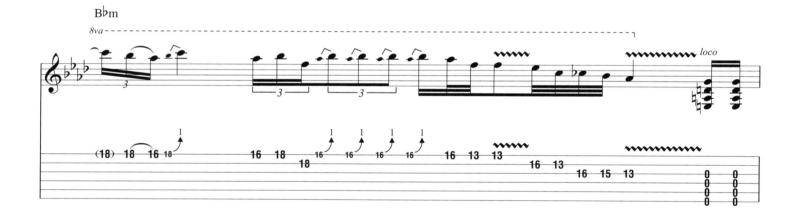

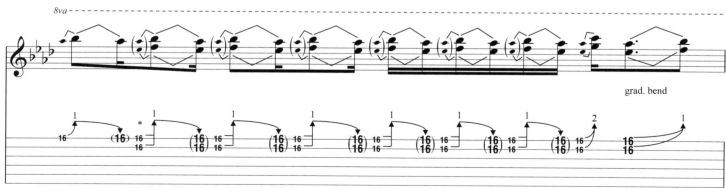

*Allow 2nd string to be caught under ring finger.

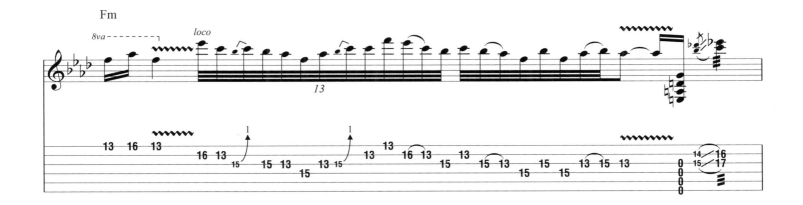

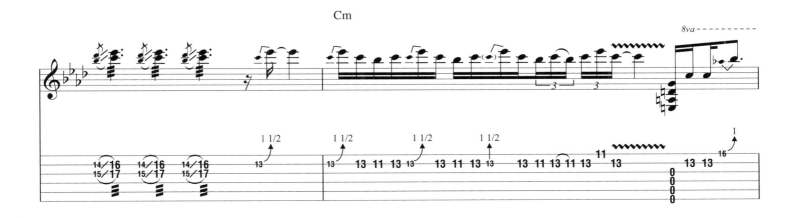

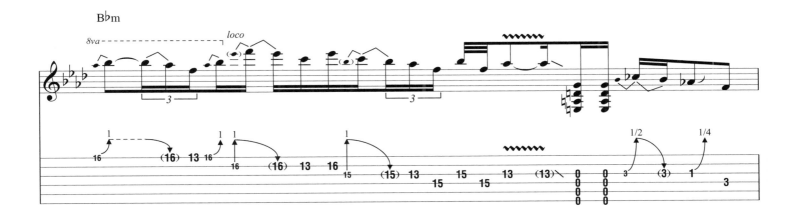

Verse

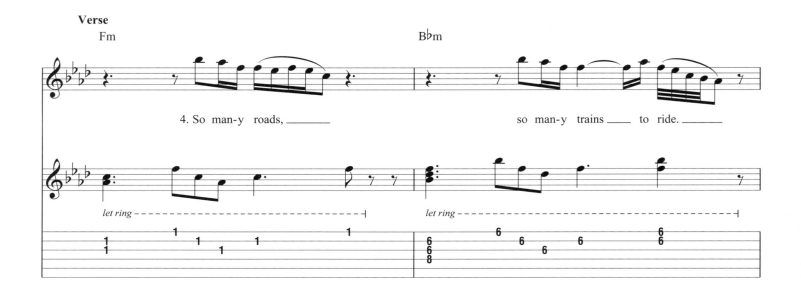

4. So man-y roads, _____ so man-y trains _____ to ride. _____

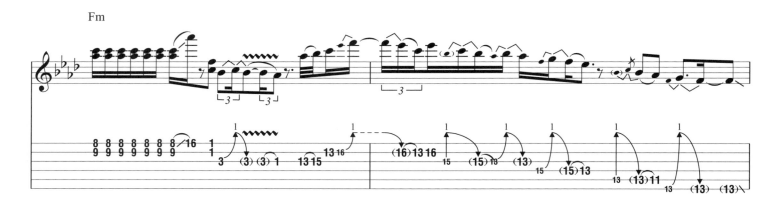

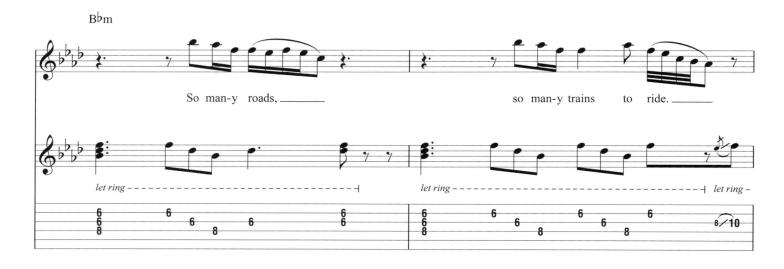

So man-y roads, _____ so man-y trains to ride. _____

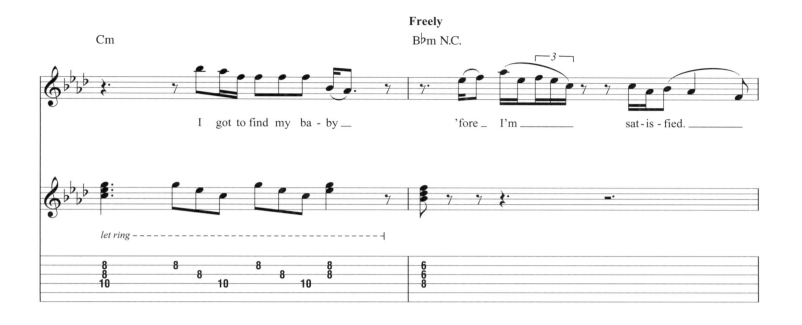

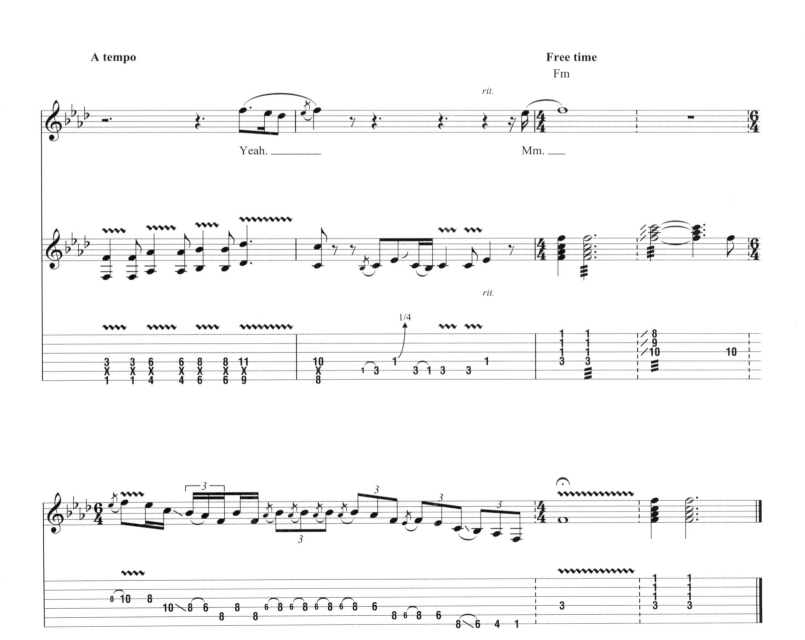

GUITAR NOTATION LEGEND

THE MUSICAL STAFF shows pitches and rhythms and is divided by bar lines into measures. Pitches are named after the first seven letters of the alphabet.

TABLATURE graphically represents the guitar fingerboard. Each horizontal line represents a string, and each number represents a fret.

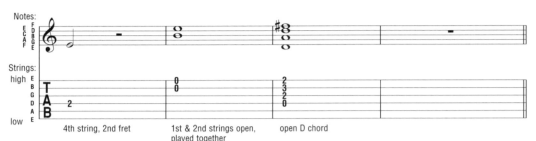

4th string, 2nd fret | 1st & 2nd strings open, played together | open D chord

HALF-STEP BEND: Strike the note and bend up 1/2 step.

WHOLE-STEP BEND: Strike the note and bend up one step.

GRACE NOTE BEND: Strike the note and immediately bend up as indicated.

SLIGHT (MICROTONE) BEND: Strike the note and bend up 1/4 step.

BEND AND RELEASE: Strike the note and bend up as indicated, then release back to the original note. Only the first note is struck.

PRE-BEND: Bend the note as indicated, then strike it.

VIBRATO: The string is vibrated by rapidly bending and releasing the note with the fretting hand.

PALM MUTING: The note is partially muted by the pick hand lightly touching the string(s) just before the bridge.

HAMMER-ON: Strike the first (lower) note with one finger, then sound the higher note (on the same string) with another finger by fretting it without picking.

PULL-OFF: Place both fingers on the notes to be sounded. Strike the first note and without picking, pull the finger off to sound the second (lower) note.

LEGATO SLIDE: Strike the first note and then slide the same fret-hand finger up or down to the second note. The second note is not struck.

SHIFT SLIDE: Same as legato slide, except the second note is struck.

TRILL: Very rapidly alternate between the notes indicated by continuously hammering on and pulling off.

TAPPING: Hammer ("tap") the fret indicated with the pick-hand index or middle finger and pull off to the note fretted by the fret hand.

NATURAL HARMONIC: Strike the note while the fret-hand lightly touches the string directly over the fret indicated.

PINCH HARMONIC: The note is fretted normally and a harmonic is produced by adding the edge of the thumb or the tip of the index finger of the pick hand to the normal pick attack.

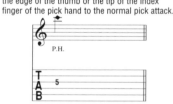

TREMOLO PICKING: The note is picked as rapidly and continuously as possible.

VIBRATO BAR DIVE AND RETURN: The pitch of the note or chord is dropped a specified number of steps (in rhythm), then returned to the original pitch.

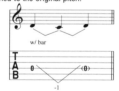

VIBRATO BAR SCOOP: Depress the bar just before striking the note, then quickly release the bar.

VIBRATO BAR DIP: Strike the note and then immediately drop a specified number of steps, then release back to the original pitch.

Additional Musical Definitions

(accent) • Accentuate note (play it louder).

(staccato) • Play the note short.

D.S. al Coda • Go back to the sign (𝄋), then play until the measure marked "*To Coda*," then skip to the section labelled "Coda."

D.C. al Fine • Go back to the beginning of the song and play until the measure marked "*Fine*" (end).

Fill • Label used to identify a brief melodic figure which is to be inserted into the arrangement.

N.C. • Harmony is implied.

• Repeat measures between signs.

|1. |2.|

• When a repeated section has different endings, play the first ending only the first time and the second ending only the second time.